PACIFIC OCEAN

UNDA STRAIT

JAVA SEA   BAN

D1643957

TIMOR SEA

INDIAN OCEAN

AUSTRALIA

ABI I.

JAVA SEA

TANJONG
PRIOK

JAVA   DJAKARTA ●

THE BELLS OF SUNDA STRAIT

THE
BELLS
OF
SUNDA
STRAIT

DAVID BURCHELL

London: Robert Hale & Company
Adelaide: Rigby Limited

First published in Great Britain 1972
Copyright © O. E. Burchell 1971

ISBN 0 7091 2481 3

Robert Hale & Company
63 Old Brompton Road
London S.W.7

Printed in Hong Kong

Ariel sings:

Full fathom five thy father lies;
Of his bones are coral made:
Those are pearls that were his eyes:
Nothing of him that doth fade,
But doth suffer a sea-change
Into something rich and strange.
Sea-nymphs hourly ring his knell
Hark! Now I hear them—ding-dong, bell.

The Tempest, ACT I, SCENE II
WILLIAM SHAKESPEARE

CONTENTS

ILLUSTRATIONS

FOREWORD

At just after midnight, twenty-nine years ago, 1 March 1942, with about one third of our ship's company I lay in the water coated with oil fuel watching our ship sinking. Exposed and helpless in the glare of searchlights from surrounding Japanese warships, she had come to the end of as violent an hour's action as was ever fought at sea. Not many minutes before I had been on board, steering her through this last battle—a vessel complex, expensive, and extremely efficient in speed and action. I had lived in her for two years and nine months, which was her whole life as an Australian warship. She had been hit by torpedoes and shell-fire had shattered her boats. The captain, just after he had given the order, "Abandon ship—*every man for himself*," had been killed on the bridge by a salvo of shells. We watched the ship go out of the searchlights' glare into the unknown blackness below, taking almost two-thirds of our shipmates with her.

Yet twenty-five years later a man left her alive.

This man was Dave Burchell. He was not a member of the ship's company but he brought back what we thought, on that night in 1942, had been blotted out for ever. This was a unique act carried out by a man of true sentiment: simply, directly, unselfishly, and at his own expense. Some few have thought that such an act might have been a desecration. In fact, nothing could be further from the truth. Most *Perth* survivors now know that Dave Burchell's sentiment, humour, and character, would have made him a most welcome shipmate in those hectic war years when men were held together by a single purpose. He has been made an honorary member of ex-*Perth* associations throughout Australia. Almost all the relics he raised are now in the National Memorial at Canberra: as a visible reminder of the ship, her dead and her deeds. The general public may have forgotten her, new generations may never have heard of her, but she has an undeniable place in Australian tradition.

Dave Burchell does not argue "to be or not to be;" he *is* and *does*. He lost a leg when young but that did not stop him joining the R.A.A.F. as an aircraftsman in wartime. He is now a diver, a no-nonsense expert to whom other divers are willing to listen. He is powerful and fit, but he is self-effacing. From his modest accounts you are apt to miss the full significance of what he has done. When the Japanese proposed to raise the *Perth* for scrap, there was a public outcry in Australia. To Dave Burchell it meant that she was in a diveable depth of water, and it would not be long before people without sentiment or conscience would be able to reach her. This book tells what happened when he decided to act. At first his prime objective was to bring back the ship's bell. In this he failed. I feel, however, that he has brought back something far more precious.

I remember how the ship, in her second-last battle, made a vivid impression on men of another navy who saw her at work. During the action of the Java Sea, H.M.S. *Exeter* was hit in the boiler room and stopped. She came under the concentrated fire of the Japanese fleet. Without hesitation Captain Waller at once took *Perth* in at high speed to lay a protective screen between her and the enemy. At the end of each leg in front of *Exeter*, *Perth* made 180-degree turns at high speed under full helm—black smoke pouring away from her two funnels, and white smoke from the smokefloats on the quarterdeck filling the gap along the surface of the sea with a dense fog. (I can still feel the ship heeling away under my feet as I put the wheel over.) Thus she made an unforgettable picture for some men. Lieutenant Hamlin, of U.S.S.

Houston, wrote later of what he saw as he looked out from *Houston*'s Number 1 eight-inch turret, ". . . there was *Perth*, a beautiful white bone in her teeth . . . three battle flags streaming . . . smoke pouring . . . firing all the time . . . rapid salvoes . . . shells falling all around her . . . *It was one of the finest sights I have ever seen.*"

Now Dave Burchell has brought back a different picture—one, because of the fatal suddenness of that night, we never expected to get. When men die at a distance from home in an unimagined place, with their bodies unrecovered and their graves unmarked, a terrible lack of finality gnaws with doubt and futile hope at the hearts of those left behind. Many will travel across the world just to see a wooden cross or a mound of earth to try to get that final acceptance. Now the bereaved of *Perth* have been given some vision of finality.

Altogether he made thirty dives, arduously piecing it all together. It is as if the ship, at last, is able to speak. He was the first man near her since the lucky ones had left her to save their lives and the rest had come with her to this faintly translucent Eden. Here, at last, was one who could take back news of those entombed when four of the eighty-seven torpedoes fired at her had hit. Now it was quiet and there was time to tell—and time to listen. She lay on her side like a mammoth resting. She looms like a towering block of buildings. In heavy weather she had often seemed tiny in a vast turbulent ocean; but in dry dock she had dwarfed the men who walked the wet barnacle-littered floor beneath her. And so she dwarfed this diver. He patiently explored, extending his endurance underwater and carefully reducing the time between dives so that he was able to make two a day. It was a calculated risk and he was never free of the possibility of an attack of the "bends."

There could not have been a better first visitor to the shrine of these dead men—never could they have been safer from desecration or vandalism. As well as fine feeling, Dave Burchell also brought uncommon skill.

The equipment had to be serviced, the compressor run, the bottles recharged, and a hundred other things done that the non-expert has no idea of. Above all it took guts and perseverance to hang on and overcome the serious set-backs he unexpectedly met.

We know now that our shipmates' grave is not a sordid one. The relics were brought to the surface and photographed wet, just as they were. And they were unexpectedly beautiful, as if encrusted with gems. Coloured transparencies will attest the accuracy of this statement. Turquoise, topaz, emerald, pearl, onyx, opal and ruby were never more vivid than these sea-wet encrustations. They cloaked the profane relics with that kind of glory John Bunyan's Pilgrim might have expected in his heaven. The whole ship must look like this—555 feet of her—and each funnel having as much area as a brig's main mast with all sail set. The whole is splashed with living colour; covered with the innocent, unprejudiced rainbow growth of animal and vegetable in harmony affirming indefeasible life-to-come. A mute sermon on the continuance of life, notwithstanding the most devastating havoc Man can wreak. The men who died so suddenly are now in a vast coffin decorated with a touching beauty which has the quality of impartial eternal justice: the significance of which, sadly, seems to escape Man as he seeks dominance and wins his successive pyrrhic victories.

Groper and other fish have established particular territories of their own now about the wreck. Where once Captain H. M. L. Waller, D.S.O., R.A.N., commanded and was killed, a large good-natured but sagacious groper now is the steadfast caretaker of the Compass Platform, the erstwhile nerve-centre of the ship in action. As I read of this in this book it seemed to me an absolutely just and appropriate succession of command after our superb down-to-earth last Captain.

Nancy Waller, the Captain's widow who has become a special sort of mother to all *Perth* survivors, gave it the nicest possible benediction when I told her about it. With blue eyes shining and a face lit from within, she said movingly, "Oh, I am glad . . . Hec would be tickled pink to know that."

Ray Parkin,
Ivanhoe, Vic.
March 1971

H.M.A.S. *Perth*

The original H.M.A.S. *Perth*, a modified Leander Class light cruiser of some 6,800 tons, was a formidable fighting unit.

She was armed with eight six-inch and eight four-inch guns, on her port and starboard sides were twenty-one-inch torpedo quads, and strategically mounted on other sections of the ship were lighter calibre anti-aircraft weapons and depth charges.

Between her twin funnels, perched high on its catapult, she carried a single-engined Walrus biplane. Known as the "Pussers Duck" by the Senior Service, not always sympathetic to this intrusion by the R.A.A.F., the Walrus, however, proved to be a worthy forerunner to her sleeker faster sisters, the Sea Furies and Sea Venoms, of Fleet Air Arm which was yet to be formed. The collective thrust of the *Perth*'s four engines, which developed 72,000 horse power between them, could drive her at speeds in excess of thirty knots over a range of 2,500 miles. Her length overall was 555 feet, and her beam 55 feet. At the time *Perth* was lost, the ship's company numbered 682 officers and men.

She began service with the Royal Navy in 1936 as the H.M.S. *Amphion*, but in June 1939 was renamed *Perth* and commissioned in the Royal Australian Navy. The outbreak of war in September 1939 found her in the Caribbean under the command of Captain Harold B. Farncomb, R.A.N.,

1. Y 6″ Turret (Trained to Port)
2. X 6″ Turret (Trained to Starboard)
3. S.1. Twin 4″ A.A. Mounting
4. After Control 36″ Searchlight
5. Crow's Nest—Masthead Lookout
6. 4″ High-Angle Director Tower
7. 6″ Main Armament Director control tower
8. Starboard Bridge Signal Projector (Recovered)
9. Port & Starboard Bridge Rangefinders (with Plow Seats for Trainer & Rangetaker—one recovered)
10. Midship Wheelhouse Scuttle
11. 2 Quadruple .5″ Machine-guns
12. Captain's Day Cabin
13. S.2. Twin 4″ A.A. Mounting
14. Starboard Quadruple 21″ Torpedo Tubes

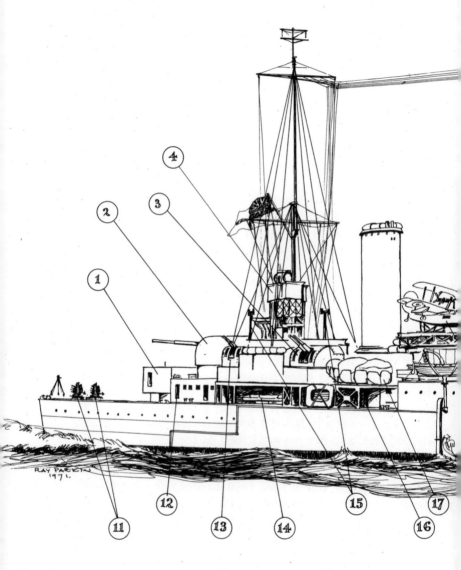

15. "Charlie Nobles"—Officers Galley Funnels
16. Space Under Boat Skids where Fire Engine is stowed
17. 35 ft Motor Pinnace
18. 32 ft cutter rigged as Starboard sea boat
19. Amphibious Aircraft on Catapult (both blown over the side in final action) Note : Crane on Port side

20. Flag Deck Starboard Signal Projector
21. Starboard 36" Searchlight
22. Starboard Bridge Lookout Positions
23. Paravane on trolley
24. B 6" Turret trained to Port
25. A 6" Turret trained to Starboard
26. Starboard Bower Anchor
27. Paravane Shoe
28. Port Bower Anchor

OUTLINE OF H.M.A.S. *PERTH*
Showing Starboard side and relevant features

and after service there and in the Western Atlantic she came home to Australia and for the next eight months carried out convoy duties in the Pacific.

In December 1940 *Perth* joined the Mediterranean Fleet as a member of the 7th Cruiser Squadron. Now commanded by Captain Sir Phillip Bowyer Smythe, R.N., she took part in the Battle of Matapan, the evacuations of Greece and Crete, and many other patrols and escorts in the area.

In August 1941 *Perth* returned to the Australia Station and, after a refit, again took part in convoy and escort duties.

Now her Commander was Captain Hector L. Waller, D.S.O., R.A.N., who had already distinguished himself with the "Scrap Iron Flotilla" in the Mediterranean, where as Captain of the destroyer H.M.A.S. *Stuart* he had won not only the title of "Hardover Hec" for his dashing and skilful seamanship, but a permanent place in Australian Naval history as a gallant and resourceful officer.

Early in February 1942, with Captain Waller in command, *Perth* again left Australia, this time for the East Indies where she joined the ill-fated A.B.D.A. (American, British, Dutch, Australian) Fleet. There, in company with such ships as *Houston*, *Exeter*, and *De Ruyter*, she fought in the disastrous Battle of the Java Sea. This battle was so disastrous in fact that when it was over, of the fourteen Allied warships involved, only *Perth* and *Houston* were left still in a fighting condition. These two ships, under orders from the Allied Command in Java, reformed at Tanjong Priok, the seaport of Batavia, to refuel and prepare for a desperate dash through Sunda Strait in an effort to escape the rapidly closing Java Sea trap.

For in February 1942, as the Japanese swept down from the North, the Allied position was chaotic. Singapore had fallen. The *Repulse* and *Prince of Wales*, pride of the Royal Navy, had been sunk off Malaysia by enemy aircraft. To the south New Guinea was being overrun, and Darwin had been bombed.

Vital information in Batavia regarding enemy movements was sketchy. What was known was bad. Only one
clear fact emerged from it all: it was obvious that in order
to escape and fight again somewhere else, the Allies had
to get out of Java . . . and fast.

As the crews of *Perth* and *Houston* hurriedly refuelled
their ships, alongside in the go-downs on the wharves
Air Force personnel destroyed stores and equipment which
had been destined for Singapore, and before they sailed
some mighty solemn handshaking took place between the
men of the ships and the men left behind in Tanjong Priok
harbour.

The latest report from Sunda Strait, seventy miles to the
West, advised that it was still clear of enemy shipping.
Consequently it was felt that if *Perth* and *Houston* could
make the Strait they would have every chance of passing
through this narrow stretch of water separating Java from
Sumatra, and reach the relative safety of the Indian
Ocean. Of course there was no way of knowing that as they
left Priok in the early evening of 28 February these two ships,
like David and Jonathon, were heading straight into the
path of an enemy invasion fleet steaming down from the
north in support of the Japanese troop landings in West
Java. As the Allied cruisers were approaching St Nicholas
Point, the northernmost tip of the island, with Sunda Strait
and freedom almost within reach, they made contact with
the enemy when from out of the black tropical night
Japanese ships appeared on every quarter.

The realisation that the end was only a matter of time
must have come to the Captains of *Perth* and *Houston* after
the first few minutes, for outnumbered and outgunned by
the numerically superior Japanese fleet, the two cruisers
had no chance of breaking through. Accepting this their
crews immediately set to, and in the true tradition of their
respective Navies, started in to slug it out and sell themselves
as dearly as possible.

H.M.A.S. *PERTH*

As she now lies sunk in Sunda Strait

DAVID BURCHELL
(Drawn to scale)

1-5. Diver's Buoy Ropes
6. Starboard Anchor in place
7. Wheel House below Compass Platform
   (Voicepipe, Saveall & Repeat Gyro recovered)
8. Starboard Bridge Signal Projector (Recovered)
9. Flag Deck
10. Catapult Structure (Catapult and Aircraft gone)
11. S.1. Twin 4" Mounting
12. S.2. Twin 4" Mounting (Shell cases recovered)
13. After Control (Secondary 6")

14. Davits of Starboard cutter
15. Starboard 36" Searchlight and Platform
16. Fire Engine (Embarked Tandjong Priok) in here
17. Quadruple 21" Torpedo Tubes
18. Captain's Day Cabin
19. Starboard Outer & Inner Propellers
20. Port and Starboard Anchor and centre line
    Capstans
21. Breakwater
22. A 6" Turret

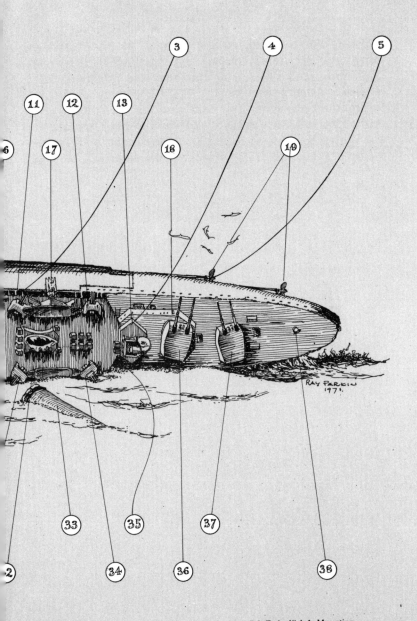

Ray Parkin '71.

Perth, who took the initial onslaught, lasted just over an hour. At the finish, having expended all her six-inch ammunition, she was firing starshells and practice bricks. *Houston* lasted a little longer. At the end she was also out of ammunition for her eight-inch guns, but was still defiantly firing .50 calibre tracers as she too disappeared beneath the dark Java Sea. Along with 800 of their men, the Captains of both *Perth* and *Houston* went down with their ships.

Birth of a Dream

A S SOON AS I'D FINISHED READING THE NEWSPAPER
article it seemed obvious that something had to be
done . . . by an Australian . . . about finding the
Perth. This was several years ago. The local press report
stated that the Japanese, some twenty years after they had
sunk the ship, were interested in salvaging her for scrap.
Apparently they had approached the Indonesian Government for permission to salvage the *Perth*, along with some
of their own vessels which were sunk in Indonesian Territorial Waters, to help pay their War Reparation debts.
But the Australian Government, outraged at the thought
of any desecration to this, an Australian War Grave, had
vigorously resisted the move, and the Japanese, bowing to
public opinion, promptly dropped the matter. However, it
did mean to me, a diver, that the ship must be at a depth
that could be reached, for the Japanese are very good at this
type of thing and must have made some preliminary

25

inquiries. As I read on, I wondered if the significance of the report would be apparent to other divers. If the information were noted in some quarters, the *Perth*'s days of lying unmolested could well be numbered, for unfortunately in this everchanging world of ours what is politically expedient today is not always so tomorrow. Also, with the rapid advance of skindiving techniques, it soon may no longer require the wholehearted efforts of a government-sponsored team to reach her. For whereas the dive using present day skindiving methods could be considered pretty dicey, it might not be long before, using improved methods, it could well be treated as commonplace. If this happened it would leave the ship wide open to be preyed on by all and sundry, including those competent but very unethical fellows, the diving pirates.

Mainly outlaw divers, these characters, for the sake of the quick quid, are always willing to take a calculated personal and legal risk to recover non-ferrous metal from sunken ships. Completely ruthless, they blast and rip with explosives and underwater cutting gear, and are quite oblivious to the desecration and ruin they leave behind. Diving pirates are shunned by most commercial and sporting divers around the world, but nevertheless many are the historically priceless artifacts that have been melted down and sold to the scrap merchant by these looters.

While the very real possibility that the *Perth*'s bell could end up as a brass ingot was totally unacceptable to me, I was at a loss, initially, to know what I, personally, could do about it. The ship lay thousands of miles away in foreign waters on the fringe of one of the world's trouble spots; no doubt the depth she was in would be extreme; and to cap it off the currents in the Sunda Strait were reported to run at up to eight knots.

"Hardly a Sunday afternoon dive," I thought, as I tossed the newspaper aside. "It's more than I could handle."

But strangely the idle act of throwing the newspaper away immediately made me feel uneasy, as if with it I were

26

throwing away as well some new found responsibility to the men of the *Perth*,and almost guiltily I quickly reached down and picked the paper up again. This unexpected reaction surprised me as I hadn't considered becoming involved, but the odd feeling that it was I who was morally accountable to find this ship first persisted, and even then, some years ago, somehow I knew I was committed.

I must admit that in those early days the knowledge of the commitment was of the comforting kind, perhaps best described as the type of feeling a young boy has when suddenly he decides that one day he is going to be a jet pilot. All he sees is the end result, with no conception of what he must go through to achieve it.

It is a time of day-dreaming, and in my case, as I slipped easily into this Walter Mitty world, I could see myself returning home proudly bearing the *Perth*'s bell. Then, with the bell safely back in Australia, installed in some suitable place such as the War Memorial in Canberra, I could rest easy in the knowledge that whatever the future held, be it foreign powers or pirates, at least part of the ship would be here, permanently commemorating the *Perth* and the men who had died with her. Like all would-be Walter Mittys I conveniently filtered out the harsh realities that such an ambitious project presented; how I was to afford the time or money—gain the necessary experience—or even start to plan it. But at that time, the time of dreaming, these things didn't matter; the time for action when they would matter was still to come. Sufficient at this stage was that the seed had been sown.

For the next few years while I certainly did not forget the *Perth*, I didn't do anything positive about finding her either. There was always some other project taking up my time, and it seems strange when I look back, but all the skindiving stunts and projects that I was involved in during those intervening years must have been preparing me for the *Perth* venture when it came.

Then, when the powers that be decided that the time had

27

come, and that I was as ready as I was ever likely to be . . . it was almost as if they opened a door.

The Reids' party was well under way when we arrived. It wasn't a large turnout, perhaps twenty or so, mainly a family affair in honour of Alan Reid, the eldest son of Cliff, our host.

Alan, a friend of mine since schooldays, was making one of his rare appearances in Adelaide from his property at Deniliquin in New South Wales, and his parents had asked a few friends in to mark the occasion.

We knew most of the people scattered round the large drawing-room, and my wife and I drifted around talking to people. After a while I noticed a chap in a wheelchair whom I hadn't met before, and I asked Alan who he was.

"Haven't you met Gordon?" he answered, surprised. "He's my cousin, Gordon Reid. He was in the *Perth*. Come over and meet him."

I downed the last of my drink and placed the empty glass on a small table near by, pausing a moment to light a cigarette before following Alan over to where Gordon was sitting. As I did so I smiled at myself as I recognised the signs—the sudden butterflies in the stomach—the slight tremble of the match flame in my hand as I lit the fag. They were signs that I had grown to know only too well. It wasn't exactly fear, although this sometimes came later, but a peculiar feeling, a mixture of acknowledgement of the inevitable and a keen almost awesome anticipation of a forthcoming physical and mental challenge.

I'd felt it the day I realised that my leg had to come off, and again, when in order to prove a point, I knew that within a month I'd have to parachute into the sea. There were other occasions, perhaps not so dramatic, but in their time equally important, and I didn't need a ton of bricks to let me know that for my rendezvous with the *Perth*, the days of dreaming were over. The time for action had come.

Possibilities

AS I HADN'T MENTIONED WHAT I HAD IN MIND TO
Gordon, he must have been irritated at the way I
monopolised his time at the party. Unfortunately
for him, being confined to his wheelchair, he found it
difficult to escape me, and all evening I followed him around
bombarding him with questions about his old ship.

Later that night I did some heavy thinking as I faced
making a decision about attempting to find the *Perth*. The
more I thought about it the greater the problems seemed to
become, and realising that trying to plan it from start to
finish in one go was beyond me, I decided just to take each
hurdle as it came. First I had to obtain approval for the
project from the Ex-*Perth* Association. Morally she was
still their ship, and without the Association's permission
to dive on her I couldn't even start to think about it.

As Gordon Reid was the President the best approach
was through him, and next day I rang him at his office and

asked if he could see me. We arranged a meeting for later that afternoon by the racecourse, and there, away from the noise of the city traffic, I poured out my story.

Gordon's initial reaction to my plan was understandable I suppose, the way I sprang the whole thing on him. But nevertheless I was saddened to see that he obviously felt I'd lost most of my marbles.

"For a start," he asked rather coldly when I'd finished, "how do you expect to survive in the currents of Sunda Strait?" When I didn't readily reply he went on, "Now look, I don't know much about diving, but I do know that the night the ship went down, the current swept men — American, Australian, and Japanese alike — down through the Strait like corks in a storm water drain."

I was a bit embarrassed as it was apparent he considered my whole scheme irresponsible, but I pressed on. "I know there are problems," I said, "but all I'm asking at this stage is for the moral approval of your Association to go into the possibilities of it."

Gordon immediately looked relieved. Obviously he considered there were no possibilities. "All right," he said, "I'll bring the matter before the attention of the members. I'll let you know their decision."

As I waited impatiently for word from the ex-*Perth* Association, I studied up on their ship. From the Public Library I obtained the book *Age Shall Not Weary Them*. It was published during the war before the story of the *Perth's* final battle was known, and while it gave a good coverage of the ship's earlier exploits in the Mediterranean, it ceased abruptly at the period in which I was most interested. The second book, Ronald McKie's *Proud Echo*, was more helpful, for not only did it give the *Perth's* last-known bearings but also the depth of water in which she sank. Buying an Admiralty Chart of Sunda Strait, and using the bearings given in *Proud Echo*, I plotted *Perth's* position. This position could only be approximate, but it did give me something to work on. The depth of water at

30

forty-two fathoms was a problem, for although I had dived deeper than this, the dives had taken place miles off shore where the currents had been relatively slight. Also, as with the bearings, the reported depth could only be regarded as approximate. What if the ship lay deeper? At forty-two fathoms, or two hundred and fifty feet, she was already nearing the limit of compressed air breathing. At that depth the associated problems very nearly outweigh the Scuba diver's ability to cope with them.

The main danger is diver's bends, for down round the two hundred-foot mark, in the half real world of nitrogen narcosis, the possibility of contracting the bends is ever at hand to claim the unwary.

While studying the Battles of the Java Sea and Sunda Strait, I learned of the U.S.S. *Houston* and the part she had played. According to the reports, although *Houston* had sunk near *Perth*, she had gone down rather closer inshore, and if this was the case it should make her the easier ship to find. I decided that if I did make it to Indonesia, I'd attempt to find *Houston* as well, and return her bell to the people of Houston, in Texas.

With this addition to the project I felt the objects of the venture rang clear enough.

The Green Light

A FEW WEEKS AFTER THE DAY I SPOKE TO GORDON REID by the racecourse, he rang and invited me to the *Perth* Association's annual dinner. The Association met infrequently as a complete group, and Gordon felt that the annual dinner presented a good opportunity to tell the members of my proposition. I'll never forget that night, not that anything really dramatic happened, but it was a rare privilege to be invited to sit down at the same table with chaps like these.

I outlined my plan, such as it was, stressing the possibility of future salvage of the ship by governments other than ours. After I'd finished and after I'd answered many questions, the members, although doubtful as to the chances of success, gave permission for me to go ahead and try. This was particularly pleasing as I'd realised all along that it was quite possible the survivors might not want me to dive on their ship. While I was fully prepared to push and shove to

TOP: The Sumantri grin, as he talks with John and the author (left) on the foredeck of the *Aries* in Priok after the diving. BOTTOM: The binnacle of the *Perth*, which is now in the Australian War Memorial, showing shrapnel holes

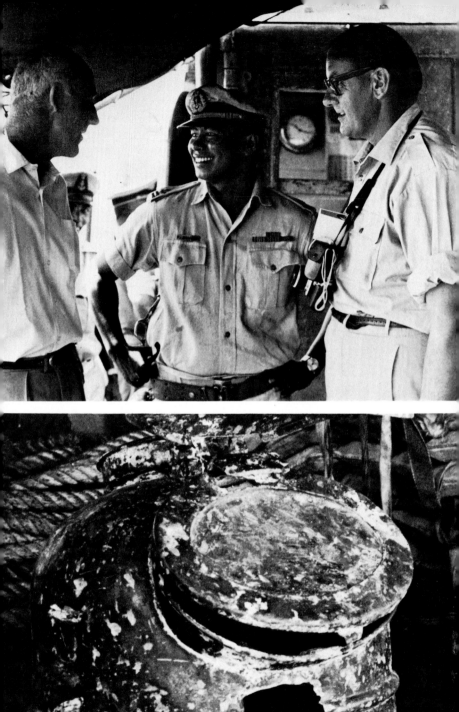

ensure the success of the *practical* aspects of the venture, on the ethical side, if it had not been their wish, I wouldn't have tried to override them.

Before officially giving me the okay, the South Australians considered it best to gauge the feelings of *Perth* survivors in at least one other state, and with this in mind a letter was sent to the Ex-*Perth* Association in Melbourne to test the reaction of the Victorian Branch. In due course the Victorians also indicated their approval, and with the moral issues cleared I went on to the next step, that of obtaining legal permission from the Indonesian Government to dive in Indonesian territorial waters.

This was a delicate matter. Since the confrontation with Malaysia, Indonesia's attitude to foreigners had been a bit touchy to say the least, and on top of this I was told the domestic situation in Djakarta, following the attempted Communist coup in 1965, was somewhat sensitive. While the political problems of Indonesia were personally no concern of mine, I realised they must have a strong bearing on the success or failure of the project. For to attempt to enlist a country's aid, when its people were still preoccupied and angry over a bloody civil war, was a job that would have to be carefully handled.

To equip me for this task in International Relations I was relying heavily on my previous experience, which was limited to once having made three friends in Fiji. This effort didn't exactly fill me with confidence, for as everyone knows, the Fijian must be rated as about the friendliest person on earth.

After considering the problem, the only solution I could see was to write directly to the Indonesian Ambassador in Canberra, tell him my story, and ask his advice. As I didn't know the Ambassador's name I rang and asked Jim Forbes, a chap with whom I'd gone to school. Jim was the current Minister for Health in the Federal Parliament, and although he gave me the information I required, he was fairly cautious about it. I think the old Forbes was concerned that

Easy does it! Transferring the *Perth*'s Starboard bridge signalling lamp from the *Aries* to the dinghy

I'd use his name, and if this assumption were correct, his concern was well founded, for I was aware of the weight his monicker would give to any request I made. Not that I compromised him, but with great care I "dropped" his name into the opening paragraph of my letter to the Ambassador, knowing full well that although it would probably incur Jim's displeasure, it must assist in obtaining me an audience at the Indonesian Embassy.

"His Excellency will see you now." The Naval Attaché's voice was soft, and combined with the marked accent, difficult to follow.

Taking a deep breath, which I hoped was disguised in the act of bending down to pick up my briefcase, I straightened up and walked past the Attaché into the Ambassador's office.

General Kosasih was shorter than I'd imagined, but both the authority and dignity of office were there. He stepped forward and shook hands, then waved me into a chair.

"Well, Mr Burchell," he said with a smile, "we meet at last. Now tell me all about this diving you want to do."

It had taken longer than I'd planned to meet the General. Not that it was his fault, for he had answered my letters politely and promptly through his Naval Attaché. But Canberra is a long way from Adelaide and I'd had to work things a bit in order to get there.

I told the General of my plans, and although he listened pretty much in silence, by the time I'd finished I sensed I had won a valuable ally. First a soldier, with politics coming a poor second, General Kosasih was naturally interested in military history, and any attempt to honour ships and men was to him praiseworthy enough to warrant encouragement.

When I started to explain my motives for wanting to find *Perth* and *Houston* he stopped me with a quick movement of his hand.

"I have visited your War Memorial here in Canberra," he said, "and I need no explanation of why you want to dive, but I am certainly interested to know how you propose to do it. Also I wish to know what assistance you require from my Government in Indonesia."

Among the papers in my briefcase was a list of items I considered as essential to pull off a dive of this nature. Its size was embarrassing. Finding the list, I handed it to the General.

"Of course, Your Excellency," I added awkwardly, "I am not expecting your Government to provide all these things, but in case some are already in Indonesia, and could be loaned, it would save my having to take them."

Feeling decidedly uncomfortable, I watched him scan the list, and as I mentally ticked off each point with him I found myself wincing, as I knew very well that most of the items couldn't possibly be taken up with me.

The list, which spelt money, time, and manpower, read:

1 A vessel from which to dive and operate
2 Recompression chamber
3 Echo sounder
4 Assisting divers
5 Winches and lifting gear
6 50-lb weights, ropes for shot lines and buoys
7 High pressure air compressor
8 Scuba cylinders

It went on to include such things as queries on diving conditions, depths, current flows, availability of stores, et cetera. By the time we reached the end of it, we were both wincing.

Desperately I cast around for the right words to say. I wanted to explain that this was not the presumptuous request it appeared, and that although some of the items could possibly be provided by the Indonesians, I appreciated that it was pretty cheeky to bob up like this and just expect them to produce the goods. Yet if they didn't, the whole project was in trouble.

I needn't have worried too much; the General was a man

of great understanding. He listened intently, then cut off my clumsy attempt at explanation with the same quick gesture of the hand.

"That's all right, Mr Burchell," he said. "I am sure our Navy has many of the things you have listed and I will recommend that they assist you. But as most of your questions are of a technical nature, my advice would be for you to go to Djakarta and carry out a survey. Talk first hand with our Diving and Salvage Command in Surabaya and see what help they are able to give you."

I hesitated at this suggestion, as I'd been hoping the whole thing could be arranged from Canberra before I left. The thought of just turning up, unheralded and unknown, and being faced with the job of trying to influence the impersonal Indonesian Navy to become interested in my plan, was not exactly what I'd had in mind.

Also the cost and time elements had to be considered, for although I owned the controlling interests in the two businesses I ran, and could reasonably expect to take the time off, it could prove a bit tough on my colleagues if overdone. Realising I was in no position to argue, I decided not to burden General Kosasih with my problems. I told him that I'd have to give the survey trip some thought, and we arranged that while I did this, he would write to Djakarta seeking the necessary approval from the Indonesian Government.

Before leaving Canberra to return home, I asked Martin Hinson, a friend of mine who lives in Canberra, to drive me up to the War Memorial. Like most Australians who have visited this place, the Memorial always has a profound effect on me. This day was no exception. As my time was short, I made straight for the Naval Gallery and spent my half hour wandering around just letting the feel of it sink in.

I'm not much of a one for making vows, but that day in the quiet loneliness of the War Memorial, in front of the painting of the *Perth*'s Captain, Hec Waller, I made a promise, and although I realised I was not yet fully aware of the size and complexity of the job in front of me, it was a promise that I knew it would take a lot to make me break.

Shortly after returning from Canberra, I could see I'd have to take General Kosasih's advice and do the survey trip. There were so many questions to which answers couldn't be obtained that I was stalemated—the survey was the only solution. Once the decision was made, I immediately plunged into a pre-embarkation whirl of visas and vaccinations, and while the bouts of smallpox and cholera raged within me, I did my best to explain to the few people who were interested that my journey was really necessary. Apparently I didn't do much of a job of it as I noticed I was far from popular in some quarters.

When the time came to catch the plane for Sydney my wife came down to the airport to see me off. Actually I wasn't sure if she came down to see me off, or to drive the car home. It was one of those days . . . I was still feeling lousy from the last batch of needles, my wooden leg was giving me some trouble, and my wife was feeling sarcastic. "Goodbye, Marco Polo," she said. "Don't worry about me and the children, just try and enjoy yourself."

Something told me that this wasn't the time for a smart reply, even if I'd been capable of one. So feeling anything but the great adventurer, with my crutches in one hand and tatty suit case in the other, I limped across to the luggage desk and silently booked in my gear.

First Look at the Strait

A S THE QANTAS JET HEELED OVER IN PREPARATION FOR its approach into Djakarta airport I decided that eight-and-a-half hours' flying in one day was plenty for me. Through the cabin window I caught a glimpse of the city below, and wondered again about the kind of reception I would receive. The plane rolled to a stop, and collecting the few belongings I had with me, I walked down the steps into the blast of heat which was Djakarta.

The Hotel Indonesia, a member of the world famous Inter-Continental Hotels chain, was huge, modern, and expensive. Room only is twenty-five dollars Australian a day—and with its additional services geared for the business executive on an expense account it was perhaps fortunate for me that I didn't intend staying long.

Up in my room I took a shower, and flopped on the bed. "Well, you're here boy," I told myself, staring at the ceiling. "What now?"

It was a good question, and while pondering it, I groped for my briefcase beside the bed and from it took a folder of papers. There wasn't much in the file, just the copies of letters I'd written to the Indonesian Embassy along with the replies, and it was the last of these that I wanted now.

The letter had arrived just before I left home, and it was important for it formed my introduction to the Indonesian Navy. Taking it from the file I settled back, and under the letterhead which incorporated the imposing emblem of Indonesia, read the typed words:

Sir,

Diving on the Wreck of HMAS PERTH

1 Since my letter to you on the 4th of April, I have received a letter from the Naval Department in Djakarta concerning your plan.

2 The Indonesian Navy will put at your disposal a boat, free of charge. However, I doubt whether the boat is equipped with an echo sounder.

3 Besides this equipment the Navy will also attach some divers to you.

4 The cost of all the operations will be your responsibility.

5 On arrival in Djakarta you are advised to contact the Assistant for Naval Intelligence at the Naval Department through the Australian Naval Attaché in Djakarta.

Yours faithfully,

M. POERBONEGORO

Kolonel ALRI

Naval Attaché

Deciding that if I could find the Australian Embassy I would also find the Australian Naval Attaché, who I kidded myself had doubtless heard all about me and was probably right now anxiously awaiting my call, I placed the file back in the briefcase.

"First thing in the morning," I said with a yawn, "it's the Australian Embassy. Right now it's a feed and early to bed."

"Sherborne," he said, sticking out his hand. "I'm the Naval Attaché. You wanted to see me?"

"Burchell," I replied smiling modestly, returning his grip, at the same time watching with interest for his eyes to light up in recognition of the name. Nothing happened.

"Er—Burchell," I repeated, frowning slightly. "You haven't heard of me?"

He shook his head. "No," he said, politely puzzled, "afraid not. Why, should I have?"

Hell, I thought, groaning inwardly and wondering where I was going to start. "General Kosasih," I suggested hopefully, like a patient father prompting a forgetful child, "Indonesian Navy—*Perth*—*Houston*."

At the mention of the ships' names the awaited flicker of interest came. "Ah yes," he said, "now I remember, you're the diver fellow. I must say I haven't heard of you through our Embassy, but the Indonesian Navy contacted me about you. Perhaps you'd better come up to my office."

Upstairs in his office Freddie Sherborne, Captain, R.A.N., like General Kosasih before him, listened to my story in silence. When I showed him the letter from Colonel Poerbonegoro he glanced at his watch.

"Colonel Sugito is the Assistant for Naval Intelligence," he said. "I know he is attending a parade this afternoon. If we don't catch him before that you'll have to wait until tomorrow." He stood up and crossing to his desk picked up the telephone. "I'll give him a ring, and ask him if he will see you now." He spoke briefly into the phone. I was in luck . . . Colonel Sugito would call at the Embassy within the hour.

"You're fortunate in having Wal Sugito for a contact," Sherborne said. "He was the Naval Attaché at the Indonesian Embassy in Canberra for a couple of years. He knows the ropes pretty well."

40

While we waited I went over the points with him that most concerned me. One thing I particularly wanted to clarify with the Indonesians was my financial obligation. "It'll be just great," I said, "if they hand me a bill at the end of the thing that I can't pay."

He agreed that this would not exactly help cement Indo-Australian relations, and promised to assist me to establish the costs involved. As we talked I started to realise the tremendous help Freddie Sherborne was going to be. Not only was he an influential ally at the Embassy itself, but being Navy he shared in the camaraderie that personnel of all Navies seem to reserve for one another, already evidenced here by Colonel Sugito's prompt response to the phone call.

When the Indonesian Colonel arrived Fred introduced us, and after the usual preliminaries we started in on our discussions.

Waludjo Sugito, a slim, dark chap in his early forties, had doubtless been assigned to the project because of his Australian experience, but as he knew very little of what I wanted I found myself having to go through all the explanations again. He also listened to my story without comment, and by the time I'd finished I was beginning to realise why they called the Navy the silent service.

Somewhat casually he scanned the formidable list of essential gear, but this time there was no need for me to worry. For Colonel Sugito, not being a diver and not particularly wanting to become involved anyway, was more than ready to palm me off on the Diving and Salvage Command at Surabaya.

"They have all kinds of equipment down there," he said. "I'll make the necessary arrangements for you to meet Lieut.-Colonel Suyatno, the O.C. He's the one to whom you should talk. When can you make the trip?"

As Surabaya was four hundred miles away in East Java the arrangements took some organising, especially as hard core Communist elements were still active in the Eastern Sector, but after a few phone calls it was fixed, and I was booked on a "Garuda" Airways flight the following Tuesday. There wasn't much more Wal Sugito could do, so after wishing me luck he left.

"Well," Fred said, after the Indonesian had gone, "you're doing all right. I don't think a foreigner has been invited into the Naval Dockyards at Surabaya since the coup."

I'm sure he meant the remark to be both complimentary and encouraging, but I had an uneasy feeling that somehow I had missed the point.

That afternoon Fred invited me home to meet his family, comprising Bobbie, his wife, and Kristen, their youngest daughter, the two older children being at boarding school in Sydney.

After lunch we went on a tour of Djakarta in Fred's car. Like all Diplomatic Personnel the Sherbornes included in their staff an Indonesian driver. This is standard procedure and, depending on your point of view, has several distinct advantages. For not only does it keep up appearances, but it provides steady employment for an Indonesian, discourages the local kids from letting your tyres down if the car is left in the street, and most important, saves the foreigner from being lynched by the mob if he becomes involved in an accident. These are not uncommon in the dense Rafferty's Rules Djakarta traffic, where young children play along the roadside in their thousands, inches from the greatest collection of wheeled vehicles imaginable.

We wound our way through Djakarta, then through the historic seaport of Tanjong Priok and on into the old city, known to the world for 300 years by its Dutch name of Batavia, but now called Glodok by the Indonesians.

Glodok these days is not much more than one of Djakarta's suburbs, and for many years a Chinatown, is now in a state of advanced disrepair. Much of the obvious charm of this once great city has faded. The water no longer flows in the choked canals, and the narrow winding streets are littered with refuse and rubble. It can be a dangerous place, and is frequently the scene of mayhem and murder, of burning overturned cars and police blocks. But we were not looking for trouble and on that bright holiday afternoon I found the place fascinating.

Asking Fred to stop the car, and disregarding the stony stares of the locals, I got out to just walk in its streets. This was my first contact with an ancient city, and it didn't take long to learn the trick of looking past the moulding unpainted exteriors of the buildings to see the classic line of the Dutch architecture. It was easy to visualise the same buildings as they must have been hundreds of years before, when Captain Cook called in to Batavia to refit his unseaworthy *Endeavour*.

Or perhaps Bligh, still coldly fuming at his treatment by the *Bounty* mutineers, had strode down this very street, rudely brushing past rich Dutch traders as he impatiently waited for a ship to take him home to England. I could have spent the rest of the day there and kicked myself for having left my camera behind.

Early the next morning, with photography in mind, I hired a taxi, and armed with the camera set off to capture old Batavia. But the police at the road block turned us back. During the night there had been a riot with several people injured, and as the driver hastily turned his car I glimpsed a blazing motorbike lying on its side . . . dark knots of people heatedly arguing. As we sped away I thought that perhaps it was just as well, as the camera lacking the aid of human imagination can record only the present, and consequently was a few hundred years too late. Batavia, that place with the nostalgic name, along with Captain Cook and the old Dutch merchantmen, was forever gone. That which remained, Glodok, ugly in title and ugly in character, like so many of our contemporary scenes, probably wouldn't have shown up too well on film.

Thanks to Freddie Sherborne I was introduced into a round of Embassy parties that defied description, mostly being held to farewell a chap named Bob Rigney, an Air

Force Major from San Antonio, Texas. Bob was on his way home after two years as the Assistant Air Attaché at the American Embassy, and as he was a popular fellow, there was a different turnout on each night in his honour. Coming from Texas he was naturally interested in the plan to find the *Houston*, and offered to fly me up to West Java so that I could study the diving conditions in Sunda Strait from the air.

Spontaneous offers of assistance like this were typical of the Americans. One night I was talking to the American Ambassador and after we had chatted for a while he asked me if I knew the *Houston*'s last-known bearings. When I told him I didn't, the Ambassador, knowing what a help the bearing would be, called Wilbur Kellogg, his Naval Attaché, over and instructed him to cable Washington and request the imformation. Also Joe Swarz, the Embassy doctor, a young Naval Lieutenant and keen student of his country's military history, offered to accompany me as medical officer and observer. With this and other offers, all looked well at the Djakarta end, but the big hurdle, that of enlisting the aid of the Diving and Salvage Command at Surabaya, was still the one that caused me concern.

"Don't tell me you're gonna dive in that?" Bob Rigney bawled in my ear as he circled the plane over Sunda Strait, and although I managed a weak grin I had to admit that the view from a thousand feet was distinctly depressing.

The fast-flowing water, apart from giving an impression of eerie depth, in some places had whirlpools on the surface that were six feet across. But I noticed that most of these were caused by the currents sweeping round the islands at the head of the Strait, and although the ships were reportedly sunk as they approached this area, they were not supposed to be near any islands. Perhaps it would be easier in the deeper water. . . .

I asked Bob to fly south down Sunda Strait so that I could photograph Toppers and Sangiang Islands, as sailors

44

from both *Perth* and *Houston* had tried to swim to them for shelter after the battle, and I knew that the survivors who had made it would be interested to see them again.

We took some good shots, some of which included the infamous volcanic island of Krakatau which had caused a major catastrophe when it blew up in the late 1800s. With the mission completed we headed for home, first across the mountains and then over the paddy fields that between them go to make up West Java.

The next day in the Australian Embassy's Landrover, Freddie Sherborne and I drove back to the same area to study conditions from the shore. As it was a Sunday, Bobbie and Kristen came with us for the ride and we had a picnic lunch on the beach in Banten Bay. Wal Sugito assigned an Indonesian Navy Major to accompany us as interpreter and guide, as some of the areas we intended surveying were remote and rarely visited.

It was a terrible trip, rough, hot, and dirty, and while not a great distance by Australian standards, the 150 miles took us nearly twelve hours to complete. Ox drays, cyclists, ponycarts, and pedestrians swarmed over the road in colourful profusion, and here in the rural areas as in the city I was struck with the same impression—people . . . people everywhere.

To the visitor coming direct from a place like Australia where the population per square mile is 3.5, to Java where the population per square mile is something like 1,120, a comparison of the relative population densities must be inevitable. Day or night, city or country, it made little difference, there were people everywhere, at times almost claustrophobic in their numbers.

One soon becomes used to it, however, and when I first returned home to Australia I missed them, and even Sydney seemed half empty.

We slowly threaded our way when the traffic was thick, speeded up when it wasn't, and stopped altogether at the occasional road blocks, although the presence of the

Indonesian Major combined with the Diplomatic Corps plates on the Landrover were usually enough for the police to wave us through.

We called on the Port Authority in Merak, a seaport at the northern end of Sunda Strait, and obtained permission to travel up the rough stony coast-road to St Nicholas Point.

To me it was all pretty exciting stuff, for not only were the people and the scenery completely absorbing, but I knew that when we reached the Point we would be within a few miles of *Perth* and *Houston*, for it was here that the battle of Sunda Strait had been fought. At the Point we stopped, and I walked down to the rocky beach to take a closer look at the water conditions. As far as I could see from the shore they weren't too bad. The current was running strongly, but the water seemed clear enough.

Deciding that the conditions would just have to be all right, I sat down and looked out over Sunda Strait. Being there gave me the same feeling I know I'd have if I visited Gallipoli — The Kakoda Trail — or the thousand other places that will always have a special meaning for Australians.

Somewhere out there under the sparkling sea were the ships. Perhaps now more cemeteries than ships, and especially because of this, it was time they were visited by the living even if only for this once, so that the report "All's well" could be taken back to those who still remembered.

Paving the Way

MY CONCERN THAT THINGS WOULD NOT WORK OUT with the Diving and Salvage Command proved to be groundless. However, during the flight from Djakarta to Surabaya, at that stage not knowing how I'd be received, I did some homework in preparation for an anticipated "hard sell."

First, I repeated Djoko Suyatno's name over and over until I'd memorised it, as the gesture in getting his name straight was about the only thing I had to offer in return for the requests I wished to make of him.

Next, after re-studying the tiresome list of essentials, I decided against asking for the loan of Scuba cylinders and the high pressure compressor. These I'd have to bring up from Australia somehow. This decision, admittedly partly based on a feeling of embarrassment at asking for too much, was also partly based on the psychological point of not wishing to appear to the Indonesians as a complete freeloader. True, the difference between the two was pretty fine, and the cylinders and compressor would be a nuisance to freight, but the effort involved in producing them would show that at least I was prepared to try and pull some of my own weight. Also, by having my own Scuba cylinders and compressor I'd be independent as far as actual diving equipment was concerned, and as past experience had taught me not to rely too heavily on other people's gear, I felt it would be unwise to take the chance, even with the Indonesian Navy.

Carefully I went over point after point on the list, thinking about them for the hundredth time . . . size and capabilities of the diving tender, how many people could live on board, would we require a base camp on shore, number and experience of the assisting divers, availability of stores and fuel. There were twenty-three major items, all more or less vital to the success of the venture, and again I was conscious of the seeming presumptuousness of the requests. All I could do was hope that the man waiting for me in Surabaya was as helpful, and in the same position to be as understanding, as General Kosasih had been in Canberra.

Lieutenant Colonel Djoko Suyatno was at the plane steps when I arrived, and after introducing ourselves we moved across to his new Holden car which was near by on the tarmac.

He was small, even for an Indonesian, and although I'm only six feet I towered above him. We climbed into the car and slowly made our way through the crowded Surabaya streets towards the Naval Dockyards. At the main gate, as the guards snapped to attention, I heard the shrill whistle of the Bosun's pipe as we passed through, and I remember feeling rather lonely and momentarily a little overawed. But by making a conscious effort I shrugged the feeling off, as this was no time to start feeling sorry for myself.

Waiting on the steps at the Diving and Salvage Com-

Members of the *Aries* crew take their last look at some of the *Perth* relics. The solid brass seat from the *Perth*'s Starboard rangefinder is predominant

mand Headquarters were three of Djoko's officers, and after he had introduced us we all set off on a tour of inspection. The Command was a huge place and Djoko, who was very proud of it, was determined I was going to see the lot. We inspected the thirty-five-foot high diver-training tanks, which were equipped with Davis escape apparatus for simulated ascents from submarines. The British Seibe Gorman recompression chambers. The rows of Scuba and conventional hard-hat gear, and then on to the compressor rooms and other miscellaneous sections that go to make up a command of this nature. It was all of great interest to me, and fortunately over the years I'd had some experience with nearly all the types of equipment the Indonesians were using. This allowed me to make the occasional intelligent remark, which of course is a great morale booster to the man who senses he is on trial.

Finally, the tour completed, we ended up in the Wardroom, and while a steward poured out glasses of cold Surabaya beer I made a last minute mental check before doing battle for the loan of the equipment I needed.

Sitting down next to me, Djoko broke my train of thought. "We are interested to know," he said, "why you, an ex-Air Force Pilot and Officer, are interested in Naval ships."

It was not the first time his direct questions had shown he knew more about me than I'd told him, but on this occasion he'd been misinformed, for although I had served in the R.A.A.F. for a while during the war, it was not as an Air Crew Officer but as an L.A.C. in the Ground Staff, and there is a difference.

Suppressing a smile at the mental picture I had of myself in the unglamorous fuzzy blue uniform of the Leading Aircraftsman, I nevertheless kept silent about the fact that I hadn't exactly won the Battle of Britain single-handed.

"Actually, finding the ships has nothing to do with the different services," I replied carefully. "I'm a diver and I'm interested in our military history. To Australians the

TOP: The *Aries* looked pretty small back alongside the *Bergamahl*, but she had done the job. The crew lined the rail to wave goodbye. BOTTOM: West Australian survivors of the *Perth* inspect the gyro compass repeater, with plug still attached by its thin brass chain, recovered from the wheelhouse

Perth is a very famous ship and we are very proud of her and her crew. It's the same thing with the *Houston* in America."

Continuing, I told them of the War Memorials in Canberra and Texas and of the attempt to dive to recover the ships' bells so that they could be sent home for safe-keeping. "I feel that we, as divers, have a responsibility to do these things," I concluded, "but as you can see I'll need some help."

A glance at the faces of the Indonesians told me that my worries were over and that I could rely on the support of the Diving and Salvage Command.

After some discussion, Djoko offered me a 300-ton sea-going diving tender complete with echo sounders, recompression chamber, and six "A" class Indonesian Navy divers to assist and act as standbys.

He was so receptive, in fact, that I was almost tempted to ask for the Scuba cylinders and compressor—but didn't. We talked the project out and finally arranged that they should meet me in Tanjong Priok harbour with the ship and divers at the end of May, allowing me a month to organise myself and my own gear.

I was highly elated at the result of the meeting, for these chaps were divers, they understood the difficulties, and their practical assistance would be invaluable. Also, with Djoko's aid the tricky navigational problems of picking up the *Perth* and *Houston* with the echo sounders would be minimised.

During the flight back to Djakarta I felt for the first time reasonably confident about the outcome of the project. Admittedly, there were still the currents and a few other things, but they could wait. At this stage the venture was looking good, and while not yet underwater, I considered it was definitely off the ground.

Back home, the inevitable crises of the next four weeks were overcome. A chap from Melbourne rang and said that four or five years before he'd seen the *Houston*'s bell in a private museum in Manila, and asked what did I make of that. I said I didn't know what to make of it. There was the difficulty involving the transportation of the Scuba cylinders and compressor from Australia. Shipping them to Djakarta was too slow, and commercial air freight was too expensive. One day in the street I told Dick Colley my problems, and he suggested I try the Air Force. "They sometimes have transport planes going through that area on their way to Vietnam," he said. "Give Geoff Giles a ring, he might be able to help you."

"Hell," I said, initially unimpressed with the idea, "I can't do that. Geoff has nothing to do with the Air Force."

Also I might say I was a bit wary of taking Colley's advice as he experienced great delight in playing on my naïve nature, and several times over the years he'd 'set me up' with his suggestions. But on the other hand he did seem to know about these things, and as I was getting desperate and couldn't think of anything myself it was probably worth a try.

Geoff Giles, M.H.R., was at a meeting when I rang his Canberra office, but his secretary said she would ask if he would speak to me. When he came on the line, being over-anxious, I must have given it to him a bit quick for somehow he got the impression I wanted to fly a party of Indonesians to Perth to pick up an air compressor.

From somewhere near the beginning I started the story again . . . this time more slowly. We had several conversations after that, the upshot being that the R.A.A.F. did have a Hercules going to Vietnam, and for the first time in eighteen months it was stopping off at Djakarta *en route*. Also, by some minor miracle, the plane wasn't fully loaded and there would be room for my gear. When the okay from the Air Force finally came through, it left two days only to road-freight the diving equipment to Richmond R.A.A.F. base in New South Wales, nearly a thousand miles away. There wasn't much time.

Gordon Wilson, the Sales Manager of the Commercial Case Co. came in and, free of charge, made up the crates to hold the gear, and two young Customs officials made the trip from Port Adelaide in their lunch hour to carry out the necessary Customs inspection. As Gordon nailed down the lids of the crates I wrote Freddie Sherborne's address on them. The Customs chaps then made out the papers and the carrier loaded the boxes on his truck. In what seemed like a flash they were gone, and hoping that the driver fully understood the complicated delivery instructions, I was left standing in the empty street seriously wondering if I'd ever see my gear again.

Apparently there was some truth in the report that the bell of the U.S.S. *Houston* had been seen in Manila. Walter Allen, my contact in Houston, Texas, in reply to the news that the bell may have been sighted, wrote advising that a reporter from the *Houston Post* had located a former citizen of the Philippines who had actually touched the bell. The Texas newspaper story ended by stating a possibility that was now also alarmingly apparent to me. . . . perhaps someone had already dived on the ships, perhaps they weren't there anymore. I didn't know what to make of it. One encouraging thing was that the survivors of the *Houston* were enthusiastic about the search, and that they would be pleased to receive any part of their ship that was recovered.

Walter Allen also sent some photographs of the *Houston*. These showed the bell's position on the main-mast just aft of the bridge, and in the event of the ship being found, would be of tremendous value.

Several nights were spent with the South Australian *Perth* survivors discussing the layout of their ship, and again we mainly used photographs. They told me that the *Perth*'s bell could be in either of two positions. Generally in port it was hung just forward of X Turret on the open quarterdeck, while at sea it was stowed inside the deck housing in the quartermaster's lobby. But no one was certain where the bell was on the night the ship sank. Even ex-Chief Petty Officer Harry Knight, although he had commissioned the ship, wasn't sure. He had gone to some trouble to draw the quarterdeck to scale for me, and although this would be a great help, I still really needed to know where the bell had last been seen.

Harry felt that if anyone should know, it would be Ray Parkin, a fellow C.P.O. and friend of his who lived in Melbourne. Ray, who had also commissioned the ship, had been her quartermaster and was at the wheel when she went down. He was a recognised authority on matters of the *Perth* and during his captivity in the ungentle hands of the Japanese and while a hundred of the original *Perth* survivors died around him, Ray sketched scenes and wrote the basic drafts of two books. Subsequently published after the war as *Out of the Smoke* and *Into the Smother*, the original manuscripts were smuggled from camp to camp under the very noses of the Japs for three and a half years.

Harry Knight rang him from Adelaide and asked if he knew the bell's position, but Ray wasn't sure either, so it looked as if I'd just have to search for it.

Because of International interest, minor though it was, and because I thought he should know something about the project in case it was successful, I wrote to the Prime Minister. The letter covered the granting of legal permission by the Indonesian Government, and the ready offers of assistance from General Kosasih in Canberra and the Indonesian Navy in Surabaya. Reading it through before posting it, I had second thoughts about sending the letter at all, realising that the Prime Minister would have one or two more important things on his mind. But I sent it off.

Several offers of assistance came from friends in Adelaide. Brian Fricker considered I shouldn't have to pay my own fare. Not that he intended doing anything practical about it, like paying for it himself, but he insisted on arranging an introduction to his friend Bert Kelly, M.H.R., a South Australian who at the time was Minister for Works in the Federal Parliament. Brian felt Mr Kelly might be able to help, but I wasn't too keen as I didn't feel inclined to front up to a Federal Parliamentarian and ask for a free airline ticket. However, Fricker arranged the meeting and Bert Kelly, who patiently heard me out, promised to see what he could do. He was as good as his word and eventually I received a refund of nearly two-thirds of the air fare.

John Martin, the President of the Underwater Explorers Club, gave me a quantity of U.E.C. Club lapel badges, and some blank membership certificates, and another friend, John Scammell, asked if he could accompany me on the trip and help out. I told him I'd think it over, but had little hesitation really in accepting the offer. For although I appreciated he wouldn't be much help underwater, as deep diving wasn't in Scammell's bag of tricks, he was a friend of long standing on whom I knew I could rely, and this alone made him a valuable acquisition.

Finally, all that was left was the last minute rush: special underwater film, flashbulbs that would stand the pressure of 200 feet, an Indonesian/English dictionary, visa problems, and finding room in my bag for a large parcel of nuts and dried fruit that Chappie Charlesworth gave me "to keep up my strength."

Cold Front

WE WERE FLYING HIGH OVER THE BALI STRAIT, AND below and to the left the volcanoes of East Java poked their coned heads through the heavy cumulus cloud indicating that at last Djakarta was close by.

Nudging Scammell, I nodded at the peaks, and he stirred, groping round his feet for his camera, at the same time keeping his eyes firmly fixed on the volcanoes like a hunter watching his prey. I understood how he felt, for the peaks contained an unreal, almost ethereal, quality which gave the impression that if you looked away, even for a second, they must surely disappear.

Soon the jet swept in over Tanjong Priok and, looking down, I noted a grey naval ship at anchor in the harbour. "Good old Djoko," I thought, "right on time." Turning towards John I said confidently, "That'll be ours, boy," and I could hardly wait to land and get started.

The next morning the phone in our hotel room rang.

It was a clerk from the reception desk advising us that a car was waiting to take John and me to the Australian Embassy . . . I recognised Freddie Sherborne's thoughtfulness. True to form, he was right on the job, and as we rode the lift down the ten floors to the ground I had a distinct feeling that this was going to be a good day. In Fred's office at the Embassy were the two crates of diving gear, and as far as I could tell without opening them the compressor and Scubas appeared to have survived their trip well enough. I was anxious to service and start the compressor but there wasn't time—it would have to wait until later, aboard Djoko's ship.

Leaving the air-conditioned Australian Embassy, we battled our way through the heat and bustle of Djakarta, this time to the Indonesian Naval Headquarters for a conference with Admiral Harijono Nimpuno, head of the 3rd Naval District, which included Sunda Strait. Wal Sugito and Djoko Suyatno were to be there also, and I was looking forward to seeing them, and to making the final arrangements so that we could put to sea.

Freddie, John, and I, received with due ceremony in the foyer, were ushered through to the Intelligence section by a Petty Officer, but as soon as introductions were completed and we'd all sat down, it was apparent that something was very wrong.

Djoko, in contrast to my enthusiastic greeting, appeared ill-at-ease and furtive, while Wal Sugito could have been likened to Pontius Pilate looking for somewhere to wash his hands. We took some time to uncover the reason for this unexpected embarrassment, but finally we found that Djoko, on thinking things over, had reversed his decision, and had officially recommended that the Indonesian Navy not become involved in the diving at all. Also his survey ship, which had engine trouble, was still in Surabaya.

At first I couldn't believe it, and quite seriously thought, with the language problems, that I wasn't hearing properly. But it was true enough. With alarming clarity, in a letter

Top: At Indonesian Naval H.Q., Djakarta. From left: Lt.-Col. Djoko Suyatno, O.C. Diving and Salvage Command Surabaya; the author; Col. Waluju Sugito, Indonesian Naval Intelligence; Capt. F. Sherborne, R.A.N., Naval Attaché to Australian Embassy. Bottom: The author points out the diving area to Commodore Wardiman (right)

to the Admiral, Djoko had explained his reasons to veto the dive . . . the depth was too great . . . the currents were too strong . . . the dive was far too dangerous.

"Imagine the repercussions," he'd asked, "if this man, who is virtually a guest of the Indonesian Government, and while using Navy equipment, got the bends, or because of the currents drowned himself?" He went on to say that in his opinion this was a distinct possibility, and that he wasn't prepared to be a party to it.

His main concern was the depth, calculated to be from 230 to 245 feet. Apparently after we had parted in Surabaya a month before, he had worked out the dive theoretically, using the Haldane decompression tables as a basis for his computations. He found that the dive was impracticable.

The Haldane tables, designed to obviate diver's bends, have been recognised as an authority for many years. But they are conservative to the extreme, and along with many other divers who have had the opportunity to purchase one, I prefer to use what is called an automatic decompression meter. Of Italian origin, the decompression meter is carried by the diver, registering the actual depth in which he is operating, and generally, using a meter, the time underwater can be doubled against the time allowed by basing a dive on tables. While I'd had some experience with decompression meters, having done several dives beyond 250 feet with them, I could hardly tell Djoko in front of everyone that he was behind the times, and a point that made me hesitate further was the frustrating knowledge that he honestly felt he was doing me a favour. However, as Officer in Charge of Diving and Salvage Command, his opinions on matters involving underwater activities were accepted without question, and it was painfully obvious that without Djoko in my team I was in trouble.

But how best to get him back on my side was a psychological problem for which I wasn't equipped, and I never really found out just what made Djoko change his mind.

TOP: In early 1942, survivors from the *Perth* used this well in the courtyard of Serang Gaol to wash fuel oil off themselves. The gaol interior is grim and forbidding. BOTTOM: Sangiang Island, looking south down Sunda Strait. Behind it is the peak of the infamous island of Krakatau

Whether the depth put him off, or that his ship was more seriously incapacitated than he cared to admit, I couldn't establish. I tried hard to get through to him, using every approach I knew, but none was successful, and although he sat in on a couple of subsequent meetings, Djoko gradually eased out of the picture, finally returning to Surabaya to go on leave. I never saw him again.

The brief popularity that I'd enjoyed before Djoko torpedoed my plans disappeared as fast as he did. In its place came a cold front, subtle at first, but becoming more and more obvious. I almost expected to see a sign on the gates of Naval Headquarters reading "Burchell go Home."

The situation at the Australian Embassy was much the same. There I'd become a nuisance causing ripples on the surface of the Embassy lake, and it seemed that my only supporters were our Service Attachés and the Americans.

Freddie did all he could, and somehow arranged for a private ship, the *Samudra*, to take John and me to Sunda Strait for three days. Unfortunately the *Samudra* had been engaged in carrying copra, and was infested with lice and cockroaches. These we didn't mind so much, but the first day out, when finally we arrived over the marks, her echo sounder broke down and I was reduced to trying visual sweeps riding the anchor chain. The visibility on the bottom was poor, and as there was quite a sea running the chain whipped five or six feet with every wave the ship rode on the surface. These violent rides caused me to lose several bits of gear, including a specially made prising tool and my weight belt. The tool I could do without, but the weight belt's loss would have been serious, so I had no option but to leave the doubtful security of the chain and go back and look for it. Finding the belt, I slipped it on and caught up again by following the grooves left in the mud and sand by the bounding anchor. I lost no time, as the chain was my only link from this eerie green wilderness to the ship high above.

After five sweeps we gave it away. This was last-resort-

58

desperation searching at its worst, with the odds stacked against any possible success, and although I realised we may have to fall back on it again later, there were one or two other methods that were worth a try first.

I asked the young Navy Captain, Sumantri, who had been assigned to us as an interpreter, if he thought some of the local Bantenese fishermen might know of wrecks. Seeking the help of fishermen was a technique we often used back home as they always seem to know where the wrecks are. Sumantri agreed it was worth a try, although he said the local fishermen used traps and nets in the shallow water, and may not be familiar with the area seven miles offshore. Also, the Bantenese were a pretty unsophisticated crowd, not even speaking Indonesian, and Sumantri, not knowing their dialect, could see difficulties in talking to them.

That night "Ming the Merciless", the name John and I had bestowed upon the Captain of the *Samudra*, took us ashore in one of the ship's boats. Ming, a real character with his half-closed slanting eyes, high cheek bones, and drooping Mandarin moustache, claimed to have picked up his knowledge of English in the saloons of San Francisco and the bars of Kings Cross. The project to find the *Perth* and *Houston* left him cold, as he reckoned it lacked percentage, but he was a good seaman and worked his ship expertly during the search sweeps.

Once ashore John, Sumantri, and I started walking. First along the built-up earth marinas stretching across the mud flats, and then on to the dirt road which wound its way through the jungle linking the coastal fishing villages. We walked for miles, slogging along in silence with the humidity bringing out the sweat, and at each village Sumantri would engage in long pow-wows with the headman, asking if anyone knew of wrecks. This was always a complicated procedure, as certain protocol had to be observed, and with the triple language problem aggravating things it was with great relief that finally we found a couple of fishermen who said they would help.

59

They also offered to paddle us back to the *Samudra* which interested me, for even though my hands were toughened after years of walking with crutches, they had so softened with sweat during the long trek that the palms were blistered and raw.

West Java can be incredibly beautiful. That night as we glided over the bay in the soft moonlight, with the lights from the cooking fires on shore and the occasional shouted call coming over the calm sea, it was at its best. My stinging hands became a minor discomfort, and I relaxed back in the warm bilge of the dugout canoe, and let them make phosphorous trails over the side. I realised at that moment how fortunate we were just to be there.

At 5 a.m. the next morning we put to sea, and Ming, following the overawed fishermen's signals, manoeuvred the *Samudra* to a point some six miles offshore. It was too far to the east for the *Perth* or *Houston* but being in no position to argue and perhaps hoping for a miracle, I dived.

There was nothing but the colourless mud and sand. Back on deck we conferred again in sign language with the fishermen . . . they pointed a hundred yards to port . . . we shifted and I dived again . . . still nothing. All day it went on, even long after we could see that the fishermen were obviously confused. Eventually we were forced to stop. My diving time for the twelve-hour period was gone, and the *Samudra* had to return to Djakarta.

On the trip back to Tanjong Priok I discussed the situation with Sumantri. Somehow I had to acquire a ship, one that was available for three to four weeks and one that was equipped with efficient sounding gear. To carry out a box pattern search, the accepted procedure when looking for wrecks in deep water, the ship would also have to be highly manoeuvrable to combat the currents. Box pattern searching is done by placing four buoys in a square about a quarter of a mile apart, the area then being methodically swept up and down with the echo sounder. If the wreck is not found in the square, the buoys are shifted across to a new position and the sweeps start again. It is slow and laborious, but is successful if the initial bearings are reasonably accurate. Sumantri promised to help in any way he could and started off by offering John and me sleeping accommodation on his ship the *Bergamahl*, which was temporarily out of commission in Priok Harbour. This was accepted with alacrity, as we had already noticed to our cost that the tariff at the hotel was as high as ever. Sumantri also promised to speak to his Commodore about a ship, although he wasn't very hopeful.

The next two weeks were among the most depressing I've ever put in, and although the old Scammell started off well enough. after a few days of my snarling he ended up feeling pretty lousy as well.

In the quest to obtain a ship I rang Admirals, pleaded with Commodores, and argued with Colonels. Each morning Sumantri would turn up at the Yacht Club wharf in his Russian jeep and hail us across the 200 yards of water to where the *Bergamahl* was moored. This was the signal to start another hot grubby day, being duck-shoved from one Naval Department to another, telling my story, and as each of these days passed the people who were prepared to listen diminished and I started to become desperate.

Finally one night, nearly three weeks after John and I had arrived in Java, unable to sleep I surrendered the stifling cabin to the bugs and cockroaches and went out on the open deck. It wasn't much cooler, but at least there was air, and I spent a couple of hours miserably staring across the stagnant water of Priok Harbour at the blinking lights ashore. Always having been a firm believer that things happen for the best, my faith was being sorely tried, for if I couldn't get a ship the next day from Sumantri's chief, Commodore Wardiman O.C. Hydrographic Command, I didn't know what I was going to do.

When Sumantri and I arrived at Commodore Wardiman's office, having left John behind on the *Bergamahl*, three or four others were already present. Waludjo Sugito, sitting at a table in the corner, was moodily scribbling with a pencil, the Commodore was talking with an Aide, and Freddie, who was faithful to the last, stood up when we entered and shook hands.

"I suppose you're sick of the sound of my name, Wal," I called apologetically to the dark figure at the table, and Sugito, showing that some Australiana had rubbed off on him during his two years as an Attaché in Canberra, replied, "I'm sick of the whole bloody thing."

He went on to say that he wasn't blaming me for what had happened, and even that morning in an effort to help he had been trying to acquire the President's barge, but he had just received advice that it had engine trouble and wasn't available. "Hell," I thought, "Soekarno's own launch, that would have been all right."

It crossed my mind to say that half the fleet seemed to be having engine trouble, but decided it was not the time, so sighing with frustration I turned my attention to the Commodore.

Wardiman and I were by now good friends, having already discussed the problem of a ship on several occasions, but today I planned a much bolder attack.

"Commodore Wardiman," I said, looking him straight in the eye, "here is a letter from Colonel Poerbonegoro, your Naval Attaché in Canberra," and then reading from the letter I quoted the clause in which the Indonesian Navy had promised to put a boat at my disposal. Glancing up at him again I continued, "Now, Commodore, I'm sorry but I want that boat." Wardiman, like most Indonesians, was a charming fellow, endowed with much humour and understanding.

"David," he admonished me with mild reproach, "you won't seem to understand. This is not my responsibility. I didn't promise you anything. I've told you before that if there were a suitable ship and it were available you could have it." We both knew he could have gone on, pointing out that with Djoko's veto the Indonesian Navy could no longer be held responsible for the promise, and that consequently the clause from the letter was completely out of context. I realised that he had purposely spared me in front of the others by not making these points, and this knowledge made what I was about to say all the harder. "I'm afraid I can't accept that, Commodore," I said, the embarrassment and rising despair making my voice sound harsh. "As far as I'm concerned you are the Indonesian Navy, you have made me a promise, and I must ask you to produce a ship. I'll settle for anything that'll float."

In the shocked silence that followed I noticed that Wal Sugito had stopped doodling, Freddie looked somewhat aghast, Sumantri had his head in his hands, and a dirty great frown had appeared on the face of the Commodore. I'm not sure now what I'd hoped to achieve with these means, as Wardiman at any time could have verbally cut me to bits. Perhaps I thought he may have been impressed with my resolute approach, I don't know. All I did know, as I sat there not knowing what next to say with the sweat running down my face, was that I'd muffed it.

But I hadn't reckoned on the Commodore. As fast as the frown appeared it left him, and he began to chuckle with genuine amusement. As the tension inside me started to break I giggled along with him, at first not knowing why, and then with the growing realisation that to him I was like a pane of glass. An exterior that he could see right through to the poor worried boob inside, one who might never make a diplomat, but who, if given half a chance, might make a diver.

"So you want a ship," he said. "Anything that will float." And with a last chuckle that should have warned me he turned to Sumantri. "Captain," he said, "as you seem to be so interested, I'm assigning you to the position of liaison officer for this project, and as far as a ship is concerned take David and show him the *Aries*. He can have that."

Bucket of Bolts

WE HAD QUITE A JOB .FINDING THE "ARIES," BUT I was so elated I didn't mind, and as Sumantri and I bumped along the overgrown tracks that threaded the Tanjong Priok backwaters I didn't even notice how quiet he was.

Sumantri had proved to be a tremendous addition to the team. Aged about thirty, he represented the new breed Indonesian naval officer, for he was alert, well trained and well informed. But the thing that probably most endeared him to John and me was his humour, for this, like his loyalty, never flagged. He spoke excellent English.

Almost reluctantly, in answer to my questions, he told me about the *Aries*. A ninety-foot Russian sloop, she had once been engaged in regular survey work. However, her sister ship had sunk with all hands somewhere off Sumatra three years before, and the *Aries*' own seaworthiness had immediately come under suspicion, hence her being "on the beach." I also rather gathered that as far as Sumantri was concerned she could stay there.

We found her resting on a mudbank in a disused canal, and my short-lived elation died at the sight, for even from a distance it was obvious . . . the *Aries* was a derelict.

Scrambling over the rusted steel deck to the small wheel-house, I squeezed inside. She'd been stripped. There was no wireless, no compass, there were no navigational aids at all. Down in the engine room sulked an ancient Russian diesel . . . it didn't work . . . the instructions were all in Russian . . . no one could read them.

I must admit that with this sudden letdown my morale did a nose dive and, sprawling dejectedly in some meagre shade on the quarter deck, I bitterly reviewed the position. From every angle it looked hopeless. On top of this, the Indonesians were embarrassed to the extreme; the Americans, although sympathetic, thought I was crazy; and my own Embassy would have been very pleased to see me fly out on the next plane.

But previous experience in similar ventures had shown that they were never easy and that they seldom went to plan. Also I don't know of anyone who has done something personally difficult who wasn't tempted to give it away at some stage.

After a while I wearily propped myself up on an elbow and toed the prostrate form of Sumantri with my foot. "Come on, Admiral," I said, trying to rouse him, "it's time we got this bucket of bolts to sea. Remember what Churchill said, 'This could be her finest hour'." But Sumantri, disgusted, tired, and unwilling to see any glory in the moment of our lowest ebb, could only reply, "Stuff Churchill."

Two days later, with the aid of most of Commodore Wardiman's engineers, the *Aries* moved, not much, but she moved. Another half a day spent re-cleaning injectors and she was ready for her sea trials . . . fifty yards up and down the canal . . . These she passed, and we had a ship. But as no echo sounder was available to carry out the box pattern searches we still had a problem, and the only solution as far as I could see was the fishermen. Sumantri agreed that if left alone in their own boats the fishermen could do better, as we both felt that working from the bridge of the *Samudra* had confused them.

It meant another long trip into West Java, but there appeared to be no alternative. As Sumantri's jeep was not capable of tackling the journey to Banten Bay, we drove into Djakarta to borrow one of the Australian Embassy Landrovers. Freddie was away in Sumatra so in his absence I asked the Consul for a Landrover. To my surprise and dismay he flatly refused. "These are Government vehicles," he said, "and you have absolutely no authority to ask for one." My explanations and arguments were in vain, he wouldn't budge, and although I could see his point the situation called for desperate measures.

With no Freddie to help, I went over the Consul's head and asked Dick Warren, the Military Attaché, to requisition a Landrover for me.

This move didn't exactly please the Consul and I was sorry, for I can't stand "smart bastards" myself, and I'm sure that this was the category in which he immediately placed me.

Back in Banten Bay we went through the rigmarole with the village headmen again, only this time they were different headmen in different villages. There seemed to be no end to it, but after some hours of verbal approaches, discussions, and withdrawals, laced with strict protocol and lukewarm tea, we found a village whose headman had actually witnessed the battle of Sunda Strait.

He was extremely reserved and not at all inclined to help, but eventually Sumantri wore him down and he promised to send some fishermen out the next day in an attempt to place buoys over the wrecks.

I gave him some money to buy the necessary ropes and weights and promised to pay each fisherman 1,000 Rupiah (about $10.00 Australian) for every wreck they could put a line on, irrespective of what the ship was. This represented a considerable sum of money to the Bantenese, who, while they lived reasonably well, were still financially pretty close to the rice line.

Although the deal appeared to have been made I was still loath to leave. I was worried that the fishermen might not appreciate the importance of their contribution, and so I made Sumantri go through it all again. We had to remember that these people were extremely insular, and that in the main they were unaware of events happening as little as five miles away. None of them had been to Djakarta, and they could only speak their local dialects. I wasn't even sure that they knew what we were talking about, but finally I had to be satisfied. Telling them that we'd be back in two days with a ship, we left.

Rice Pudding?

INLAND FROM BANTEN BAY IS THE WEST JAVANESE TOWN of Serang, known only too well by the survivors of the *Perth* and *Houston*, for it was here in the notorious Serang gaol that most of them, after their capture by the Japanese, had started their terms as P.O.W.s. Some had died there, the rest after an anxious few weeks were transferred to the Bicycle Camp, as the gaol in Batavia was called, for eventual distribution to various other hell holes all over Asia. The road back to Djakarta passed through Serang and I wanted to photograph the prison as I knew the *Perth* survivors would be interested to see it again.

Sumantri wasn't at all keen on the idea, as apparently in Indonesia entering a gaol is not considered to be very smart, even if one goes in voluntarily, and when I first suggested stopping he rolled his eyes in despair. . . . It had been a long day and this was about the last straw.

Scammell, who had been tremendous during the past

68

three weeks—unobtrusive, but always there when wanted —also thought I was being too ambitious. He was quite blunt about it. "Hell boy," he said, "you wouldn't even be allowed into the Adelaide Gaol, especially with a camera, let alone up here. They'll probably think you want to stir up trouble with the political prisoners and we'll all be invited to join 'em."

But it seemed it was worth a try, so prodding the unwilling Sumantri into action we drove round to the District Director's office to have a go at obtaining the necessary permission.

The District Director turned out to be a reasonable chap who, once he understood the reason for us wanting to enter the gaol, immediately gave the okay, but back at the prison gates it was another story, for the Warden, a suspicious character, took some convincing.

Finally he let us in, but only after he had relieved Sumantri of his .45 automatic and posted half a dozen armed guards around us. There was some doubt about whom they were protecting, us or the prisoners, so rather quickly we took the photographs of the grim interior, and then, thanking the Warden, we set off again on the slow hot trip to Djakarta.

It was well after dark even by the time we reached the outskirts of the city, and driving to the Embassy we picked up Sumantri's jeep, but before going on to our own 'prison', the *Bergamahl* in Tanjong Priok Harbour, we called at the hotel to see if there was any mail.

Walking through the huge plate glass doors into the air-conditioned luxury of the pub was like entering another world. It seemed incredible that this had been ours only three weeks earlier, and standing dirty and tired by the reception desk, John and I felt almost belligerent towards the clean, well-dressed business men who drifted from the dimly lit bar to their expensive evening meals in the restaurant alongside. At the desk there was a letter for each of us, plus a note to me from Freddie.

69

My letter, which was from my wife, also contained messages from our four daughters.

Jane, the eldest, started off,

> Dear Father,
> I hope you are very successful in your search to find the bells of the H.M.A.S. *Perth* and the *Houston* . . . for your sake and ours.

Mandy, the second eldest, asked me to bring her home a tape recorder from Singapore for her birthday, and Cassie, the youngest, just hoped I'd get the bells. It was our third daughter, Susan, whose message depressed me the most. She wrote:

> Dear Daddy,
> I hope you are feeling well. I have not had a bad day at school. Please try hard to get the bells. We are all depending on you, so get the bells please. Sorry it is not a long letter but I cannot think of much.
> Goodbye for now,
> Yours truly, Susan
> P.S. Remember we are depending on you.

"Starve the bloody lizards," I thought, "that's just great." But it got worse.

John's letter, also from his wife, informed him that his son Mark had broken an arm at school, and Freddie in his note, written before he left for Sumatra, suggested I write to the Indonesian Government relieving them of any responsibility in case I drowned myself.

Although not great drinkers, Scammell and I decided it was about time we socked a couple. Collecting Sumantri we were half way to the bar when I realised we didn't have any money. I'd given all I'd had on me to the village headman in Banten Bay.

We straggled dispiritedly towards the door but as we

70

were about to go out we ran into Geoff Giles and John McLeay, another South Australian M.H.R., on their way in.

This unexpected meeting was the cause of much celebration, and not only did we spend an hour or two in the bar at the parliamentarians' expense, but it was like blowing a safety valve to relax for a while and talk of things other than our own particular problems. Geoff Giles and John McLeay were on their way home after several weeks in Vietnam, and as they also came from Adelaide there was plenty to talk about.

Later that night we bade them a rousing farewell, and feeling quite rejuvenated, Scammell and I sang bawdy Australian songs to Sumantri all the way back to the ship.

As I understood it, part of my contract with the Indonesian Navy was to provision the *Aries* for her three to four weeks' voyage, and as she had a crew of twelve, plus John and myself, the provisioning represented quite a project in itself.

I brought up the matter with Commodore Wardiman, intending to ask his advice on what to purchase for the Indonesian sailors, but he wouldn't hear of it. "You don't have to feed the crew," he said, "that's our responsibility. But unless you want to eat rice all the time you're out there, you had better obtain some food for yourself."

I'd found out, when buying food for our trip on the *Samudra*, that the only place to purchase suitable tinned stores in Djakarta was from the Embassy canteen, but this had posed no problem as Freddie Sherborne was President of the Canteen Committee and had let me use his account.

Thanking the Commodore for his generosity and agreeing that John and I wouldn't want to survive on rice for a month, I asked him for the loan of his jeep so that I could go into the city and buy food from our Embassy. This didn't exactly thrill the Commodore as he wanted to use the jeep himself, but he let me have it on the condition that I was

71

back within the hour. It didn't leave much time, as we could easily spend half an hour stuck in a Djakarta traffic jam, so with all haste I grabbed a driver and took off.

"You can't use the canteen without a Diplomatic Passport," he said. "The trouble is you chaps come up here and think you can take over the place." In Freddie's absence I was running foul of the Consul again. I sighed. He was probably right, no doubt there were rules and regulations that governed these things and in a way it embarrassed me to have to push him like this, for he was really a decent enough fellow.

"But can't I use Captain Sherborne's account?" I asked. "I'm sure he wouldn't mind, you see I've used it before." But the Consul's reply clearly indicated that I was wasting my time. "Not without his authority," he answered primly, and I could feel the anger start to stir.

I knew that most of the Embassy staff gave me no show of finding the ships, and that to them I was just a bloody nuisance causing unnecessary trouble. This was fair enough, and as much as possible I'd tried to keep out of their way, especially as it could put Freddie on the spot, and after all he had to live there. In retrospect one realises that no party is all right or all wrong, and that in the black and white of the picture there must always be shades of grey. But unfortunately the Consul was my countryman, and because of this I felt the restraint which I'd been forced to exercise towards my hosts during the past weeks did not apply to him.

This time I couldn't contain my frustration and anger, and like most people who lose their temper, I proceeded to make a fool of myself, telling the official a few home-truths, and for a grand finale, although I forget now where I suggested he put it, I rudely told the Consul to "stick his canteen."

Back in the jeep I lit a cigarette and morosely contemplated the position in which I'd placed myself. It boiled

TOP: As the *Aries* anchored in Banten Bay, fishermen canoed out to say that they had hooked a wreck. BOTTOM: The fishermen's village. The influence of Dutch architecture had penetrated even to this remote spot

down to the fact that while there had been some satisfaction in my talk with the Consul, I still didn't have any stores, and unless I thought of something pretty quickly, Scammell and I would be facing up to some fairly uninteresting meals.

There was really only one alternative worth trying, so giving the slumbering driver a nudge I asked him to take me to the American Embassy.

"Lieutenant-Commander Carr, please," I said to the girl at the desk and as she turned away to ring him I did my best to smooth out my crumpled and not very clean shirt.

Jim Carr, the American Assistant Naval Attaché, had been very good to John and me, asking us over to dinner a couple of times and generally taking an interest. He now represented my last resort on the food front.

"I'm sorry," the girl said coming back to me, "but Lieutenant-Commander Carr is in conference and won't be able to see you for some time."

"Bloody hell," I muttered, but the thought of eating nothing but rice pudding for a month urged me on.

"Would you tell him it's Dave Burchell," I said, forcing a smile and trying to make the name sound interesting, "and it's most urgent!" I could see she was unimpressed, but reluctantly she rang again. This time Jim Carr said he would see me.

Up in his office Jim introduced me to his two visitors. One was a chap from State Department Washington, the other was a submarine Commander from Vietnam, and as I sat down with them Jim handed me a cup of beautiful American coffee. "Do you know what this crazy Australian is trying to do?" he said with a laugh, and went on and told them of the diving in Sunda Strait. "Tell me," he concluded, "have you got a ship yet?" I explained the *Aries* as best I could, and how because of the lack of echo sounders we had made arrangements with the fishermen in Banten Bay. "Don't discount the value of the fishermen," the Washington fellow said. "It was a fisherman who found the atomic

Top: After each dive, John and the author (left) entered the main points in the diving log. The black instrument in front of the author is the decompression meter, which determined when it was safe to dive again. Bottom: Freddie helps to clean up relics. In the background is H.M.A.S. *Jumbuck;* the name given to the dinghy because the mother ship was *Aries* (the ram)

bomb that was lost off the coast of Spain, even after the Metal Anomaly Detectors and other modern searching gear had failed to locate it."

"Also, keep an eye out for oil slick," the Commander added. "There is still fuel oil coming up from the *Arizona* in Pearl Harbour, and she was sunk over a year before the *Perth* and *Houston*."

This encouragement, although not much, represented about a hundred per cent improvement on what I'd been getting and I thanked them. However, being conscious of the limited time left with the Commodore's jeep, I thought it best to come straight to the point.

"I have to provision the ship, Jim," I said, "and it's only fair to tell you that my own Embassy won't have a bar of me, but can I buy some stores from you blokes?"

Carr laughed again. I could see I was making his day. "Is that all you want?" he asked with a grin. "Sure, help yourself, book it up to my account, you can fix me up when you get back."

First Find

ALTHOUGH WE HAD BEEN UP FOR OVER AN HOUR IT WAS still dark when the ropes that moored the *Aries* to the *Bergamahl* were slipped, and we slowly made our way past the brilliantly lit Pilgrim ships that formed the roads into Priok Harbour. In a way it was just as well, for the rusty unpainted old *Aries*, with twenty-seven life-jackets tied to her rails, would have presented a sorry picture in the daylight. As far as I could see the only reason we had twenty-seven jackets was that there wasn't room for twenty-eight, for I'd got the distinct impression that the crew were not overconfident in their ship.

Scammell, whose cautious approach to nautical matters back home had won him the title "Captain Tuna . . . the Chicken of the Sea," made no bones at all about how he felt, and for the first week he even slept in his life jacket.

Also, although we didn't know of it at the time, Commodore Wardiman's conscience got the better of him to the extent that he detailed an officer to follow us along the coast in a jeep, his job being to view our progress continually through field-glasses and to report back immediately if the *Aries* disappeared.

As we cleared the harbour, Sumantri mustered all hands on the small fo'c'sle as I wanted to tell them what was going on. There were two officers, three petty officers, and seven seamen, and as none of them could understand English Sumantri spoke for me. As he warmed up to the subject he got a bit carried away, but perhaps it was a night for the dramatic. For this was Tangong Priok, one of the most historic sea ports of the world, and our course, set to thread initially through the vast Bay of a Thousand Islands, was following the long gone wakes of those two other ships whose unmarked graves we were now about to try to find.

Sumantri told the men that the eyes of all Australia were upon them, and that it was their duty as Indonesian sailors to assist in every way possible to make the search a success.

Listening, I looked around at the dark intent faces dimly reflected in the light from the wheelhouse, and it seemed that John and I were a long way from home, not only in miles but in time as well. It was very moving, and to me not over-dramatised at all, for although our boat was old and ill-equipped, and we were relying on the memories of a few simple fishermen, somehow I felt confident and I knew we would succeed.

Late that afternoon we arrived in Banten Bay, and as the *Aries* moved in behind Pandjang Island several dugout canoes, or prahus, as the Indonesians call them, came out to meet us. First aboard the *Aries* was the headman. He told Sumantri that his men had located a wreck and that first thing in the morning they would take us out to where they had placed the buoys. From what he said the position seemed too far to the east, but it was a start.

None of us slept much, for it was hot and steamy close inshore where we'd anchored. To me the night appeared interminable. Lying on a mattress on the *Aries* foredeck,

I lay awake and worried. Still wound up from the effort of getting here at all, I felt I couldn't relax even though we were back at the diving area. True the ship had made the seventy mile journey, but how long would she last? Already there was an uneasy growling noise coming from her gear box and we'd found that most of her other equipment was either badly worn or broken. Finally, telling myself I was worrying about things that were beyond my control anyway, I thought, "Ah well, to hell with it, if the ship breaks down, it breaks down. We'll worry about it then."

As it turned out, although plenty of other things broke, the old *Aries* engine with its groaning gear box at no time let us down, and never once during the three weeks we were out there did the Russian diesel miss a beat. Part of the credit for this phenomenon must go to the Russians, who designed the thing in the first place. But part must also go to the two Indonesian engineers who, sweating it out in the claustrophobic hot box that was the *Aries* engine room, alternatively coaxed and bullied the revs out of her.

Cautiously the helmsman edged the *Aries* up to the fishermen's buoy. Looking down from the comparative safety of the deck, I felt a strong affinity for the yellow painted drum as it strained half submerged against the current, for it reminded me of a tired swimmer struggling to keep his head above water.

"Well, what do you think," Sumantri asked as he squatted down beside me. "Do you want to leave it for a while? The current may ease up in an hour or so."

I knew this was possible but it was also on the cards that it could be even stronger, as this was our experience on the *Samudra* when initially we'd tried working to the tide tables. Either we couldn't calculate them correctly or the tables were wrong, for each time the current was meant to be slack it invariably was running a banker. I'd already decided to disregard the currents as much as possible and couldn't see any point in hesitating now.

77

"No," I replied, "we won't wait, let's see what they've hooked." Putting on my wet suit was a minor ordeal in itself. I couldn't remember ever having been so hot, the humidity was intense, the thick nylon-lined rubber of the suit suffocating, and by the time I was geared up, complete with boots, gloves, and hood, the sweat was running in rivulets. The reason for the full wet suit was not for warmth, its usual function, but for protection against coral and sea wasps, whose sting can be fatal. Also, a full wet suit has a buoyancy factor of about ten pounds in salt water, which is handy if an accident occurs and the diver has to swim on the surface for a prolonged period, for by dropping the weight belt you can float indefinitely. Along with the usual standard equipment I was also using an S.O.S. decompression meter, an oil-filled diaphragm-type depth gauge, a Rolex Submariner watch with lapse time bezel, and a heavy diver's knife which was in a sheath strapped to my leg.

The three Scubas we'd brought up from Australia were 72 C.F. "Seabees," fitted with tensile type pressure gauges on the regulators so that I could tell at any time, by sight or feel, the remaining air pressure in the cylinders. As we always used the dinghy when diving, we took one of the spare Scuba sets with us. The third was always kept on board the *Aries*.

Wasting no time once over the side of the dinghy, I started the haul down the cable, which because of the current angled at about forty-five degrees and quivered like a piano wire. The water was dense with vegetable matter and plankton, which not only cut the visibility back to about ten feet, but also made the cable slippery and difficult to grip. At a hundred feet by the depth gauge, I was winded and my arms were so tired from pulling that I started to wonder what would happen when I'd have to let go. Levering forward I managed to rest after a fashion by hanging with my arms over the cable, and there I was stuck, too weary to go up or down. The only consolation I could think of was at least the boys back home couldn't see me.

After a minute or two the hanging by my arm pits became so uncomfortable that I had no option but to move, and I pulled on down, slowly passing the 120-foot mark, then 130, with another brief stop, and on again. At 160 feet, suddenly, a ship materialised all around me out of the grey fog.

Apparently I was so engrossed I'd moved right into her without noticing the usual sign that a wreck is near, generally evidenced by the school fish attracted to the food provided by such an artificial reef.

Momentarily confused, I scrabbled for a footing on her canted deck and as my foot came down, something large and slimy clawed from under me. It was a four-foot green turtle and as it frantically sculled away into the gloom, although there was no chance to discuss the point, it would have been a toss up who had received the biggest fright.

The ship, which was a freighter, was lying on her starboard side, and because of the shell holes and other visible damage it seemed likely that she was one of the Japanese troop ships sunk by the *Perth* and *Houston*.

Letting the current take me, I skimmed across the deck up the bridge. It was burnt out, with the still visible scars graphically indicating the fury and pain of her sinking. From the bridge I swam over her foredeck to the bow and then worked back aft. Even after all these years there was still evidence of the hasty departure of the crew. Her life boats were gone, with the exception of one whose smashed remnants were still hanging from the twisted davits. The anchors were still in place and the holds were packed with trucks and equipment.

Moving along the guard rail, I went over the stern and swam down to her single propeller. It was a big skinny looking screw, with blades about seven feet long, and looking at it I couldn't help wondering again about that night when this propeller, along with so many others, had stopped its turning for ever. I was struck with a feeling of sadness and would have liked to stay on and investigate this

79

unknown ship, perhaps identifying her, as no doubt someone would be interested, but there was no time. Gliding with the current, I made my way back to the midships section and the shot line.

On the way I did manage to salvage one of her porthole rims and, although the glass was gone, being solid brass it seemed to weigh a ton and was difficult to carry.

At the shot line I started working to free the weight at the end of the cable, but found it was inextricably caught deep inside the ship. This presented several problems, for it not only meant the loss of one of our precious weights and about forty feet of cable, but as I had nothing with me to cut the wire I would have to go back up to the *Aries* and get a hacksaw. I wasn't overjoyed at the thought of the return trip, but there was no option, as we couldn't afford to abandon the 200 feet or so of cable from the wreck to the buoy on the surface. Also, instead of just tying the porthole to the weight and letting the chaps in the dinghy pull it up, I'd have to carry it, as once the cable was cut and the strain released, the severed end could fly anywhere. I gave the wire a couple of savage jerks, but it wouldn't budge.

Carefully I placed my arm through the rough, marine-growth encrusted porthole and hoisting it up on to my shoulder, started the angled haul back to the surface.

The second trip with the hacksaw wasn't much better than the first, but apart from nearly being decapitated when the cable suddenly parted after I'd all but despaired it ever would, and a lonely "blind" swim back to the surface, the job was done.

On reaching the top, I found that the current had swept me some distance from the ship. Fortunately my old mate Scammell was awake, he being more interested in what had happened to me than the crew who were engrossed in unravelling the tangled cable, but in spite of his prompt action, by the time they picked me up I was exhausted and quite content to lie gasping on a mattress on the *Aries* foredeck.

"There she is, chaps" On a chart of the area, the author shows survivors of H.M.A.S. *Perth* the spot where their ship now lies

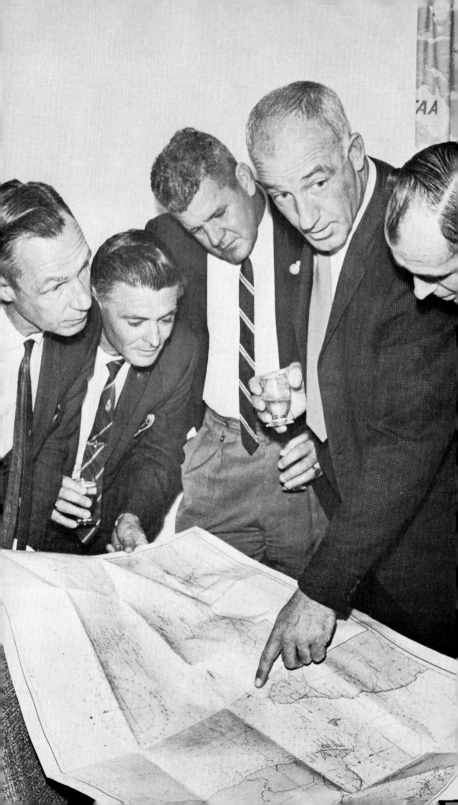

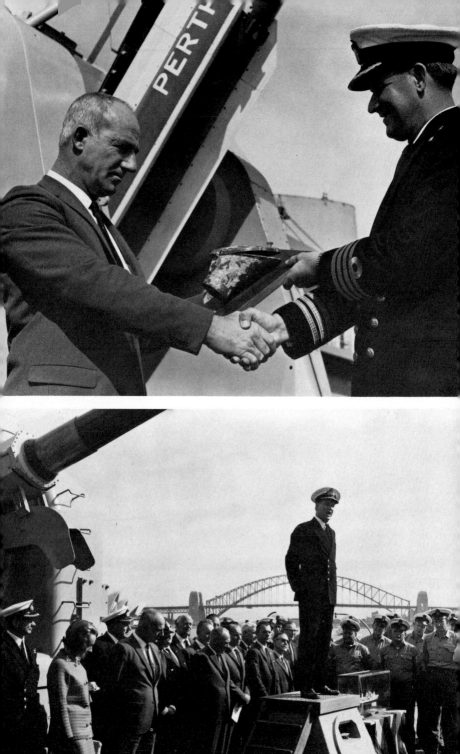

Sumantri, whose already evidenced interest in mattress-bashing had moved John and me to nickname him the "Kapok Kid", flopped down beside me. He lit up a fag and stuck it in my mouth. "Well, Daddy," he asked, "what did you find?" He'd called me "Daddy" ever since I'd shown him Susan's letter saying she was depending on me.

"It's a freighter," I replied, puffing on the clove-scented Indonesian cigarette, "probably a Japanese troop ship. Would you thank the fishermen and tell them this is not the ship we're looking for. Ask them what else they've got."

He ambled off aft with the message, engaging in a brief scuffle with John as they passed each other in the narrow waist of the *Aries*.

Scammell had been working on the porthole recovered from the freighter, and as he carried it forward I could see he'd already cleaned most of the marine growth from it. Closer inspection showed why I was able to break the rim away from the ship's bulk head so easily. About half the circumference was sharp and jagged where the heat of the fire had melted the brass, and fortunately the mountings securing the frame to the ship were nearly gone.

We entered the dive in the log, noting the bearings and describing the ship as an unidentified Japanese troopship of about two to three thousand tons.

"The fishermen say there is a big ship about three miles further to the east," Sumantri said, collapsing again. "Do you want to move over to it?"

"Three miles to the east," I exclaimed, exasperated and experiencing an uneasy feeling at the increasing enormity of the search. "Hell, that will place us about seven miles from the *Perth*'s reported bearing. Haven't they anything a bit more to the west?"

Sumantri shrugged. "That's all they seem to know of," he replied with a yawn.

"Okay, let's go," I said, sitting up and stretching, "but don't hurry. According to the decompression meter I won't be able to dive again for about five hours."

Top: A proud moment. Part of the old ship officially becomes part of the new. The author hands over the voice tube mouthpiece to Capt. D. Leach, C.B.E., R.A.N.; captain of the new *Perth*. Bottom: Captain Leach addresses the ship's company before receiving the presentation. N.S.W. survivors of the old *Perth* stand behind him

Six-inch for Sure

THE BANTENESE FISHERMEN NEVER CEASED TO AMAZE me the way they could drop on to a wreck with visual bearings. Over the years I'd had enough experience at it to know just how difficult this medium can be, where the slightest error can mean ending up hundreds of yards off target, especially when the cross bearings are a mountain or a headland twenty miles away. However, to these chaps it was a piece of cake, and full of confidence they manoeuvred their dugouts to the required spot.

After about half an hour of battling with the current, the second wreck was hooked with one of my spare weights attached to a thin nylon line, and when all was ready I again went over the side of the dinghy. The current had increased to an estimated five knots and as much as I tried I couldn't pull down against it. The thin nylon line kept slipping through my hands and finally I was forced to give it away, not even being able to get under the surface.

Winded, I hung on to the side of the dinghy and talked the situation over with John. He suggested we leave it and come back in the morning when the current should be less strong, but I was all for trying again with a thicker rope. However, at that moment the weight of the loaded dinghy proved too much for the light line, and with a twang it parted. At this sudden release the dinghy took off heading down Sunda Strait with the *Aries*, after a slow start, as she had to turn round, in hot pursuit.

By the time we arrived back over the wreck everyone was pretty sick of the deal, but I badgered Sumantri into asking the fishermen to try again as I was anxious to identify the ship which I felt was another freighter so that we could leave it and work more to the west. After some trouble manoeuvring, the fishermen again hooked the wreck, this time using a half-inch diameter rope and a ten-pound shot. The day was very hot, and even underwater it wasn't much better, for the sea was warm and thick, with the porridge-like plankton sticking to the rope, making it slippery against my rubber gloves.

At about 150 feet the school fish started to appear, and I knew I was nearly there. The fish, which were grey, with yellow backs and tails and about eighteen inches long, hung in thick clouds. I stopped to check my instruments and make a routine survey. All was well and I started off again, cautiously, eyes probing ahead and around for signs of the wreck.

For a while nothing, then from out of the grey mist a ship started to take shape under me. At first it was just a confused pattern of steel plates and rivets, and I couldn't recognise any more or form a mental picture of how she was lying. Moving on, I realised the ship was on her port side and that the weight at the end of the line must have caught on something beyond her.

The visibility was improving, now more than twenty feet, and I could make out the shape of her propeller with the rope leading straight to it. This was better than I'd hoped,

83

for once on the propeller it should be easy enough to find hand-holds to work back to the hull.

The last few feet were like a nightmare, the propeller wouldn't seem to come any closer no matter how hard I pulled against the current, and I was just about finished by the time I moved in behind the protection of the huge blade.

After a while, I stood up on the drive shaft and inspected the propeller. It was larger than the one on the freighter we'd found that morning, with the blades more clover shaped. Taking hold of the edge I peered out into the current, immediately springing back, in my haste almost losing my footing. There was a shark pack gliding along in line astern making straight for me!

They were heart stoppers, and I don't mind admitting that the sight of them chilled me to the marrow.

Pressing back against the blade of the propeller I watched as they circled, counting them. There were six, and each one looked lean and fast and had cold swivelling eyes. I reckoned that I was safe enough where I was, but I couldn't stay there. The only escape from the sharks seemed to be the rope, stretching away into the fog across the hull. It looked awfully open and unprotected, and after first checking my air supply, I looked quickly around for possible alternatives.

It was then, almost at the limit of the visibility, that I saw the second propeller. I experienced a chill far more sudden and severe than that brought on by the sight of the sharks. This was no freighter! Twin propellers on the starboard side could mean only one thing . . . This was a four-screw ship, a warship, and the only warships in the area were the *Perth* and *Houston*.

For a moment my mind was numbed, and crouching down on the shaft I stared at the metal without really seeing it, rubbing at it with my hand and blinking unbelievingly. It was all too quick to comprehend. I was like a boxer who had mentally conditioned himself for a hard, fifteen-round bout, only to find that he'd won by a knockout in the first.

As my mind cleared there came a feeling of almost over-powering awe at the knowledge of where I was, together with a strong sensation of trespass which made me doubt my right to be there.

But this was a natural reaction, and was as it should be, and I knew that if I were going to finish the job this psycho-logical hurdle had to be overcome like any other problem. I looked again at the drive shaft, this time seeing it in detail. Which one was she? The question seemed to leap at me. Was this the *Perth*'s outer starboard prop I was on, or was it one of the older, but larger *Houston*'s? I had to know the answer. A check of my air supply and instruments showed I had another ten minutes. With luck there was time.

There was still the shark pack, but my attitude towards it had now changed. Having found one of my ships some-how gave me courage. The sharks were the intruders, not I, and by the time I was ready to move I'd worked up a hate against them.

To reach the hull I had to cover ten feet or so of open water, so waiting for a break in their picket line I leapt across. Unfortunately, one of the sharks had got out of sequence in its circling, and as I sprang from behind the protection of the blade we very nearly collided. My Karate-like yell was a hundred per cent fright, despite my new-found courage, but it served its purpose and the shark nearly slipped a disc in its effort to avoid contact.

Working slowly up the hull, using anything I could find for hand-holds against the current, I noticed the sharks' interest was much less aggressive, and by the time I'd reached the deck line they had disappeared altogether.

Grasping the edge of the deck, I peered through the porridge-like sea at the superstructure. It was eerie and ghost-like in its stillness, and difficult to identify. Although realising that because of its size and complexity a quick identification may not be possible, I started to move aft in the hope of finding something specific. Without any real purpose in mind I casually looked upwards and for the third

85

time that morning I froze. Above me, like two dark outstretched arms, were the guns.

I knew the *Perth*'s guns were twin six-inch and that the *Houston* had triple eight-inch. From where I was I could only see two, but couldn't be sure. There may have been a third beyond my visibility. Working farther aft until I considered the angle was right, I pushed off upwards from the deck, and by swimming hard across the current just managed to rugby tackle the starboard barrel as I was swept past. For a moment or two I lay there, catching my breath, then worked my way along the barrel to the muzzle.

The bore was nearly choked with coral, and I remember that as I looked inside the barrel a small blue fish popped out. Measuring the bore against the back of my hand confirmed what I think I already knew . . . it was six inches. We had found the *Perth*!

Gropers and Octopus

D URING THE NEXT TEN DIVES I MADE SURVEYS, USING
the knowledge gained to form a mental picture of
the ship. The huge bulk of her made this task
difficult, for being nearly 200 yards long and 100 feet from
keel to compass platform the *Perth* was nearly the size
of a city block, and with the visibility down to twenty feet
I found it hard at times even to work out where I was.

But we kept at it, first placing several buoys along her
whole length, finally ending up with five. These were
spaced at about 100-foot intervals, and when each new
one was in place I'd dive and survey that particular area.

It was slow and frustrating work. The ropes we were
using for shot lines were old and rotten, and the first two
mornings we found that during the night the ropes had
broken and that the buoys were gone. The fishermen would
obligingly find the wreck and we'd start again. After
finally deciding that the ropes were useless, we spent time

87

unravelling the steel cable used for the dive on the freighter. This held all right, and we started to build up the row of buoys again.

Eventually the completed mental picture obtained showed that the *Perth* was lying on her port side, with her bow strangely enough pointing east back towards Djakarta, and away from Sunda Strait and the freedom she was so desperately seeking.

Deep in the starboard side of her hull, approximately under A turret, there was a gaping hole about forty feet across, but the rest of her visible side was undamaged, with even most of the glass still intact in the scuttles.

The six-inch turrets were all in place, with A turret's guns trained forward, the starboard gun elevated, and the port gun depressed. B turret was trained hard to port with the gun muzzles stuck in the sand, and on the quarterdeck X and Y turrets were pointing about forty-five degrees to starboard. Up forward, her anchors were in place, and the characteristic cruiser bow still swept down in one clean unbroken line. The "Walrus" aeroplane had gone, but the retrieving crane with its open-web steel work was lying on the sea bed beside the ship.

On the four-inch gun deck the barrels pointed in all directions, with S2 turret at least having received a direct hit, as several live rounds, bent at right angles, were lying inside.

The port torpedo quad was under the ship, and I couldn't reach it, but on the starboard side the four tubes were empty with the muzzles slightly trained out, and in some of the places I rubbed with my glove, the brass work was still shiny under the thin film of calcified marine growth that covered it.

On the deck near the aft control was a vehicle that I first took to be a truck, but which turned out to be some sort of fire-fighting unit. I inspected its tyres; they were Dunlops and still seemed to be inflated.

On the upper bridge the damage was more evident. The

standard compass and most of the other navigational instruments were gone, and there were several shell holes in the deck.

Along the front of the bridge the groups of voice tubes showed shrapnel damage, but the row of stainless steel handles for winding up the weather screens were untouched, and glinted dully through the grey green water.

The bridge held a strong fascination for me, and I never tired of spending time there visualising the scenes that must have taken place on it. The spit and polish of the peace time days, when as H.M.S. *Amphion* she was one of the most up-to-date cruisers in the Royal Navy. The desperate times, when as a member of the 7th Cruiser Squadron she had distinguished herself so well in the Mediterranean in the battles of Matapan, Greece, and Crete. The less hectic period of convoy duty in the Pacific, and the final days and nights in the Java Sea. In my imagination I could see her various Captains and other personnel, who had lived, fought, and at the last died, on this small patch of deck.

On the starboard side of the bridge, growing from out of the guard rail and defying the current, was a magnificent spray of Gorgonia coral. It was over six feet across and because of the depth it looked grey in colour, but in fact was probably orange or dark red. I was always careful not to damage it, for although the ship is now still, and the mortal remains of the men she took down with her have long since gone, I felt the coral spray represented a living tribute to the memory of both the ship and the men.

After the survey dives were completed we began a serious search for the bell.

The position in which the ship was lying meant that the Quartermaster's lobby, in which the bell was meant to be kept, would be right underneath her, and the first approach was to try to move in under the port side of the quarterdeck and find the door leading inside the ship.

With this in mind, I swam down over the four-inch gun

89

deck to the sea bed, and then worked aft along the quarter-deck housing. There was a gap about three feet high between the built-up sand and what had been the top of the quarterdeck superstructure, and swimming through this I entered a restricted cave-like area right under the ship.

Inside, it was dark and still, and I was conscious of the 7,000 tons of ship on top of me. Also I missed the bustle and company of the current. However, when my eyes had grown accustomed to the gloom I could see there was company of a different kind, and I warily watched the three or four large groper whose home I'd invaded.

Contrary to popular opinion, tropical groper, while being big and ugly, are not normally dangerous. But they are unpredictable, and it would have been unwise to upset them in the confined area we were sharing, as they were bigger than a man, and probably weighed well over 300 pounds. Waiting quietly, I watched as one by one they moved away into the black recesses of the ship, and when finally satisfied that they had gone I turned over and started a close inspection of the quarterdeck housing, which was now acting as a ceiling to the cave.

Being out of the current's cleansing influence the weed growth was more prolific under the ship than on the open areas outside, making the search for the door into the lobby difficult. Working carefully over each square foot, I slowly moved deeper and deeper under the ship, not realising that my progress was being watched with interest, and no doubt growing alarm, by yet another resident of this quiet eerie backwater. During a routine check I glanced over my shoulder, and found I was practically eye to eye with a very agitated octopus.

Unlike the groper which can be almost stupidly curious, the octopus is generally extremely timid, and if given half a chance will jet smartly off when disturbed. But unwittingly I'd backed this chap into a corner, and he had nowhere to go. For a moment or two we regarded each other. He was big and evil looking, and from the tentacle that was nervously flicking out I estimated he was all of twenty feet across. There was never any question as to who was going to give way, and cautiously I backed off, deciding that the door to the lobby wouldn't be in that direction anyway.

In the attempt to find the bell I made six separate dives in under the ship. The groper soon became accustomed to the intrusion, finally taking no notice of me at all, and at times in the cramped area I even bumped into them. Only at my touch would they move haughtily away, their huge down-turned mouths registering disapproval, like a group of dowagers disturbed at their afternoon tea. I didn't see the octopus again but I knew he was there, and in my imagination I could feel him watching, and wondered if I worried him as much as he did me.

The area was lonely and claustrophobic and not without danger, and it was always with a feeling of relief that I'd leave it when my time was up, and swim out through the narrow opening into the relative brightness outside.

I found the door on the fourth dive. It was closed tight with all the locking handles dogged. I tried time after time to open it, using a hammer and crowbar, but couldn't, and finally I was forced to accept the fact that as far as I was concerned the *Perth*'s bell was irretrievable.

To get so close, almost within a few feet, and not be able to reach it was a great disappointment, But we had no option, and reluctantly I decided to leave the quarterdeck to concentrate on other areas, in the hope of finding suitable artefacts to take back home.

John was pleased enough at the decision, for although he, too, was disappointed about the bell, he was never keen on the dives under the ship. His only indication that I was okay during his anxious waits up in the dinghy was the sight of my bubbles hitting the surface. But when I was under the ship these would be trapped, and he would have no idea for ten minutes or so of how I was going, and if in his opinion I stayed a bit too long, I was always sure to get a verbal blast as he hauled me back on board.

For the first week, after the diving for each day was completed, we would return inshore and anchor in the small bay fronting the village of our two fishermen. Gradually the villagers' initial shyness disappeared until finally John and I were accepted as part of the scene. We found they were friendly, simple people, but that they had their own strict code of ethics, evidenced the day Sumantri told me that our fishermen, Salim and Makri, wanted to leave us and go back to their fishing. As we didn't really need their help anymore, the *Perth* being now securely buoyed, I said "Okay, ask them how much I owe them."

Sumantri grinned, as if anticipating the question. "They don't want any money," he said. "They say that as you have worked so hard on this they want to be part of it as well. They have talked it over with the headman, and that's their decision."

I was mighty impressed. Although the money was not a large sum by our standards, it was more than the fishermen could hope to save in twelve months. We had given them small gifts and cigarettes, but not knowing their language had made it difficult to communicate. I think the fact that they realised the importance of the dive pleased me more than anything else, for I knew that with this knowledge, the appreciation to them of their own contribution must naturally follow.

"Hell, that's tremendous," I said to Sumantri, "but they can't afford to do that. Tell them I appreciate their thought very much, and that without their help the *Perth* would never have been found, but that I insist on paying them."

Feeling that the fishermen's departure warranted some recognition we dressed the ship, draping the red and white flag of the Republic of Indonesia across the front of the wheelhouse, and set up the compressor crate as a table on the foredeck. All the boys turned out in their number one uniforms, and with Sumantri acting as interpreter I made a speech of appreciation to Salim and Makri.

After giving them the money, which I'd discreetly placed

92

in an envelope, I also presented them with an old pair of Fletcher Jones pants, my dark glasses, fifty kilos of rice, and some soap. By the time John dobbed in a couple of shirts and a tube of Golden Eye ointment, for Salim's conjunctivitis, they thought they were made. To round it off I made them both members of the Underwater Explorers Club, taking great care to write their names correctly on the certificates.

Salim replied, thanking us for the gifts, and stating that he and Makri would always be ready to help us, and amid much handshaking we put them ashore on the beach at their village.

South from St Nicholas Point down Sunda Strait is the large seaport town of Merak which we made the home base for our operations. It was here that we refuelled, maintained contact with Djakarta over the Port Authority's telephone, and purchased fresh provisions from the well-stocked markets. Merak was also the turn around point for the two ships that daily ferried the thousands of travellers crossing the strait between Java and Sumatra. I could never find out just what caused this mass commutation of people, but guessed that with a population of over 120 million a few would always be on the move.

One ferry the *Bukit Barisan*, named after a mountain in North Sumatra, arrived every morning, and the other, the *Krakatau*, would arrive in the afternoon.

They were both sizable ships of about 1,000 tons, and were invariably loaded to the gunwales with passengers. As there was only an hour and a half allowed for the turn around, it didn't leave much time to unload the six hundred people and freight, and reload for the return trip. But everyone lined up three wide in a cheerful queue, and in no time it seemed they were all loaded and the ferry would be gone.

At the wharf in Merak one day the ferry *Krakatau* had loaded her human freight and was ready for the trip across

93

the strait to Sumatra. She gave the usual blast on the foghorns indicating she was about to cast off, and apart from wincing at the noise as we were tied up in front of her, we took no notice.

It was only at the unaccustomed second two blasts that we looked up from our work on the *Aries* and saw that a prahu, which had been heading down Sunda Strait for Merak, was now at anchor with sails furled, and was lying across the entrance to the small harbour. She was blocking the *Krakatau*'s path and the Captain, who was an impatient man, was telling the crew of the prahu to shift.

But they took no notice, and her decks remained deserted. Up on the bridge of the *Krakatau* the Captain produced a heavy sub-machine-gun and without any fuss or further warning started firing bursts into the water a few feet off the prahu's stern. To this there was an immediate response, and as the crew swarmed all over her, the prahu's anchors were up and the sails unfurled in the blink of an eye. But even then she didn't move fast enough to suit the Captain and as she slowly got under way, in an effort to assist, he kept "boring it up her" with the machine-gun.

As the bullets whizzed over our heads, Scammell and I, along with the rest of the crew, lay flat on the *Aries* deck. We caught each other's eye and Scammell grinned. "Hardly the Manly ferry leaving Circular Quay," he said.

The travellers on the ferries intrigued us, and John and I never tired of watching them as they filed past. Generally we were refilling the Scuba cylinders on the *Aries* foredeck, and I suppose with the diving gear lying around we were of as much interest to them as they were to us. Sometimes they asked a question of our crew, obviously inquiring who we were, and the sailor on watch would answer in Indonesian with "Australie" being the only word we could pick out.

I was sitting on the wharf in Merak patching the knee of my wet suit one day when Sumantri sat down opposite.

"Do you live here?" he asked politely. I nodded.

"Yes," I replied, "My name is Daddy. I was born in Merak. It was many years ago, even before the little yellow men came."

"I suppose you think I'm just a simple fisherman," he continued idly, throwing pebbles into the water. I agreed that he certainly looked simple, but he carried on as if not hearing, at the same time drawing his right leg up under him.

"Actually, I'm 007 Dave, the famous one-legged Australian skin diver," he said, "no doubt you've heard of me." He could continue in this vein indefinitely and we were always exchanging identities.

Another time as I was recuperating after a particularly hard dive, he came up to where I was lying on the mattress and swooping down plucked a clump of hair from my chest. Oblivious to my surprised yell he inspected the hair closely.

"What's this," he asked, puzzled, "Australian wool?"

Resignedly I relaxed back again. "Yes," I said, "and what's more it's AAA quality."

"Is that so," he exclaimed in an interested tone, then selecting one of the few hairs growing on his shin, he pulled it out, and offering it to me he said proudly, "Well, this is Indonesian nylon."

Styke

WE SOON SETTLED INTO A ROUTINE ON BOARD THE *Aries*, this being timed around the two dives a day that I was able to make. Early each morning after leaving Merak, we'd head up the Strait to the diving area, the idea being to get the first dive in by seven o'clock, so that a second could be made at about one or two. Then in the mid-afternoon, with the diving for the day finished, we would return to Merak and while the crew refuelled the *Aries* from one of the ferries, John and I would fill the Scuba cylinders with the compressor. Generally our first indication that another day was about to dawn was when the cook's off-sider placed a mug of thick Javanese coffee on the deck by our heads. One sip of this and the eyes involuntarily snapped wide open. Once I made the mistake of drinking some at night, paying for it by lying awake for hours until the effects had worn off.

The meals that John prepared from the American stores

Mr Veryard, then Lord Mayor of Perth, Western Australia, inspects Freddie Sherborne's cap. In the foreground, beside the 4-inch shellcase, is the cap of Lieut.-Commander J. Carr, U.S.N. The caps and shellcase now hang in the Mayor's Parlour, in Perth Civic Centre

H.M.A.S. PERTH
SUNK DURING THE BATTLE OF SUNDA STRAIT
BY A HIGH SWELL CAST UP BY THE SEA
AND RECOVERED FROM THE
HAVE REMOVED
THE OLD ROTTEN
JULY 2ND 1967TH

were pretty terrible. It wasn't entirely Scammell's fault, although I don't think he'd win too many Oscars as a chef, but the rations were short and we had to augment them with large dollops of rice to eke things out.

In an effort to give the rice a bit more kick, but to the horrified fascination and disbelief of the crew, he would mix apricot jam with it, and sprinkle cut up bananas on top. We didn't think it was too bad, but to the Indonesians this bastardisation of perfectly good rice, the staple diet of countless millions of Asians, was beyond the pale, and although we offered them some on numerous occasions, not even Sumantri would touch it. We sent one of the *Aries* officers, Lieutenant Àbdul Kahar, to Djakarta with the news that the *Perth* had been found. Apparently I had been forgiven by the Australian Embassy, for upon his return we found that with the congratulatory messages were four tins of condensed milk.

Sumantri also left us for a few days, as he had been recalled to Djakarta by Commodore Wardiman to report on our operations. This left us without an interpreter, as no one else in the crew could speak English, but with the Australian-Indonesian dictionary that I'd bought before leaving home we got by.

The main problem I found was in the pronunciation of words, for while the Indonesian is very staccato in his speech, Australians, although we deny it, tend to drawl and use the broad "a". I'd already had a couple of instances of this. Once was when Djoko Suyatno asked me my first name. When I told him it was Dave, he said delightedly, "Well, that's appropriate, Dive the diver."

Another time was during my first trip to Djakarta, when after ordering a meal in the restaurant at the hotel, I introduced myself to the chap sitting opposite, adding that I was an Australian.

"You didn't have to tell me where you came from," he said in a heavy American drawl. "As soon as you ordered your 'styke' I knew you were an Australian."

Top: Mr Ed. Clark, then U.S. Ambassador to Australia, received the other half of the *Perth*'s 4-inch shellcase on behalf of the people of Houston, Texas. Bottom: This porthole rim is now the property of the W.A. Branch of the Navy League, and is kept at the H.M.A.S. *Perth* Memorial Hall at R.A.N. Base, Leeuwin

While I gave the Yank a big cheerio for his trouble, I was forced to accept the fact that apparently we do have an accent, and to make the crew of the *Aries* understand me at all, I had to change my pronunciation dramatically. A word like Djakarta for instance, that in Australia we would pronounce Jar-car-dar, the Indonesians pronounce Ja-cot-ta. They also fool around with their "ues" and "oes" and mostly the "d" is silent altogether.

Every afternoon the men would gather on the tiny foredeck, and with the aid of the dictionary and many drawings, I'd tell them what had happened during the dives that morning down on the *Perth*. By the time Sumantri came back we were getting quite good at it, and he was rather put out when we jokingly told him he wasn't needed any more.

Exploring the *Perth*

THE FIRST DIVE DOWN THE NUMBER ONE BUOY CABLE revealed that the shot at the end of the line had pulled clear of the ship and was resting on the sand some ten to fifteen feet off the *Perth*'s bow. Kneeling on the sea bed I heaved at the heavy weight in an effort to shift it back. It wasn't that the weight itself was so heavy, but the current dragging at the buoy on the surface and the attached 300 feet or so of cable made it difficult to handle.

Finally I decided to leave the shot where it was, and turning my attention back to the ship, curiously studied the unfamiliar head-on view. I remember being struck by her enormous bulk. For the bow, rearing up from the sea floor like some huge canted cliff, disappeared out of sight into the fog above, completely dwarfing me.

On impulse I decided to try and swim the complete length of her. The current was right, and if the distance proved too great, and I ran out of time, I could ascend any one of the four buoy cables between me and the stern. Then once on the surface it wouldn't be difficult to attract the attention of the crew in the dinghy, who could abandon their position at the number one buoy and pick me up.

Pushing off from where the *Perth*'s bow dipped into her keel I worked diagonally across the hull, skirting the torpedo hole under A turret and making the deckline at a point just aft of the starboard anchor. To the left ran the neat row of scuttles along the ship's side, and following these I moved on aft. About the position of the Seamens' Mess Deck I started peering into each porthole, but the inside of the ship was dark and still and I couldn't identify anything specific.

I thought of Perc Partington, a real character, who now lived in Adelaide. He had been a bandsman in the *Perth* and just before I left home he said, "If you do find the ship, go to my locker on the Mess Deck. There's a hundred quid in notes in it."

I didn't think there would be much left of the money by now, although when a friend of mine, Mac Lawrie, dived on the U.S.S. *Peary* eighteen years after she was sunk in Darwin Harbour, he brought up all sorts of odd things. Included in these were some old 78 r.p.m. phonograph records featuring the Andrew Sisters, and although the records were warped and a bit scratchy they still played.

Leaving the row of portholes, I swam up past B turret, pausing a moment at the turret's open door to reflect on who perhaps had been the last to use it a quarter of a century before, and to wonder further if this unknown sailor had survived the holocaust that must have met him as he stepped outside. From B turret, with the current behind me, I soared up the front face of the Bridge structure, past the open scuttles of the wheelhouse, up and over the compass platform weather screens and on to the bridge itself.

As I sat down on the brass plow-type seat of the starboard rangefinder, I noticed that it moved slightly and I made a mental note to come back on a subsequent dive to see if it could be recovered.* But realising that I'd have to keep moving as I'd only covered about a third of the ship's length, I let go of the rangefinder and the current picked me up again. Together we swept the length of the bridge and then over the flag deck, where I angled down across the flow and again stopped by grasping one of the two davits that once had held the starboard cutter but which now stood empty from out of the ship's side.

Moving on past the mid-ship section where the forward deck line steps down to the waist of the ship, I made another quick inspection of the fire-fighting unit which was jammed in behind one of the characteristic lattice-like supports for the deck above. From this point I crossed back over the upper deck to see if there was any trace of the Walrus aeroplane that had once roosted there, for I'd promised Jock McDonough, the pilot of the Walrus, that I'd try to find his plane and if possible bring part of it back for him. But although I searched the area where it should have been for some time, there was no sign of the gallant old crate. It must have been swept away by the force of the water, pouring and tearing over the hull, when the *Perth* made her last plunge.

However, the heavy recovery crane, used for retrieving the Walrus from the sea after her chancy flights, was lying on the sea bed beside the ship, and I swam the length of it in the hope of finding some small part that I could take home for Jock. But the crane's construction of open-web steelwork offered nothing readily removable, and I had to leave it empty-handed.

Just as I was about to swim back to the main hull my attention was attracted by a large smooth object to the right, which not only towered above me but disappeared out of sight in both directions along the sea floor. Moving towards it I approached with caution, for somehow its

* A few days later I managed to work it free, and the seat is now in the Canberra War Memorial.

very shape and smoothness made it appear foreign, causing me for some reason to become suspicious.

It was not until I was right up to it that I recognised what it was and snorted with amusement at letting my imagination run away with me, for the ominous looking object was nothing more sinister than the aft funnel.

Following the funnel out along the sand to its end, I grasped the rim and peered inside. It was surprising to see the mass of pipes that nearly filled it, as I'd always thought of a ship's funnel being a hollow tube like a factory chimney. It now provided a home for dozens of small fish, which darted nervously back at my unexpected appearance, and as I watched them swim around in their snug apartment, I thought of the workmen on the Clyde who had originally made this thing of rivets and steel. Even in their wildest imagination, they could not have had any conception of its ultimate use.

Making my way back along the top surface of the funnel I was surprised to see that a large spotted ray was accompanying me. He was about ten feet across, and although his sudden appearance gave me a start, I couldn't help but admire the grace and ease with which he moved. The ray, soon bored by my slow awkward pace as I battled with the cross current, left me to plod on alone, and I was thankful enough to reach the ship again and make use of the handholds her superstructure offered.

Passing over the four-inch gun deck I inspected the torpedo quads underneath it, noticing that the four tubes still retained a certain look of deadliness which even the encrusted covering of coral failed to hide.

Reaching the quarterdeck I drifted with the current, looking upwards until the guns of X turret came into view. It was here that I'd first joined the ship when I came up over the side from the propeller, and which ironically was the same place that Harry Knight told me he'd left her twenty-five years before.

On the starboard side of the quarterdeck is a door

leading into the passage which once serviced the Captain's cabin and the wardroom. The door is open and the passage, now more like a lift well because of the angle at which the ship is lying, is dark and choked with debris. I didn't realise it at the time, but this door corresponds with the one for which I spent so much time searching on the port side.

Apparently the two doors are linked by the passage, for although it angles around in places and involves a couple of water-tight bulkheads, it does run from one side of the ship to the other.

Perhaps it is just as well I wasn't aware of this, as I would have been tempted to use the passage in an effort to reach the bell, and although I could have possibly cleared a path down it and taken a shotline with me to have something to follow on the way out, it may have been foolhardy to attempt it on my own. Especially as it had already been established that at least one octopus was in residence in the area.

Turning away from the door I checked my air supply and instruments. They showed that it was time to leave and I moved across to the number five buoy cable and started the ascent. About twenty feet up I stopped and looked back, and I realised how much my feelings toward this ship had changed since our first meeting.

Initially she had overawed me, for then she reminded me of a famous woman, known to the world as a proud and well-groomed beauty, but who at the peak of her fame had completely disappeared under a veil of mystery from the world scene. Then twenty-five years later, with her looks gone and her hair tangled and matted, she had suddenly, unwillingly, been rediscovered. Maimed and caught unprepared, she was unable even to raise her head from the mud or flee from the curious eyes of this unexpected intruder, and I was embarrassed for her.

But during subsequent dives this impression altered as I learned to see in her a new and different kind of beauty.

103

For where once it had been Carmen-like in its flashing fierceness, now her charm was of a calmer nature, and where originally it had been her function and duty to destroy life, now like an oasis in this sea-bed desert her whole being supported it.

If anything, rather than being embarrassed, I was now even more proud of her.

Top: We say goodbye to our fishermen, Salim and Makri. Still clutching their newspaper-wrapped parcels of presents they are made members of the Underwater Explorers' Club. Bottom: The bronze gyro compass from the wheelhouse

The elusive *Houston*

O NE AFTERNOON, JUST BEFORE THE FISHERMEN LEFT, we were sprawled in the shade of a verandah in their village. Wishing to start the search for the *Houston*, I asked the headman if he, or any of his people, knew of other ships sunk in the vicinity of the *Perth*. With Sumantri acting as interpreter they listened intently as I told them of the *Houston*, and of how this great ship had come to be in their waters.

Originally the pride of the American peace time fleet, the *Houston* had also been a favourite with President Franklin Roosevelt, and was often called the "President's Yacht" because of the many holidays he spent aboard her.

Shortly before Pearl Harbour, the *Houston*, which was the flagship of the American Asiatic Fleet, left Shanghai for the Philippines, but when the Japanese landed she was forced to withdraw to Java. Initially, as she steamed south to escape the enemy, she was in the company of

TOP: A voice tube mouthpiece from the bridge, before the sponge and marine growth was cleaned off. BOTTOM: The *Aries* bow wave washes over the oil slick made by fuel oil seeping up from the wreck. On calm days the oil slick is spread for miles by the currents

her sister ships *Boise* and *Marblehead*, but was left to run the gauntlet on her own after these two cruisers were put out of commission by Japanese aircraft.

Under almost continuous air attack during the lonely trip, her commander, Captain Albert Rooks, eventually made contact with the Allied Forces in Java, and the *Houston* joined the A.B.D.A. Fleet, a hastily thrown together group of American, British, Dutch, and Australian ships, doomed to failure it seemed because of language and communication problems.

Following the battle of the Java Sea during which the ill-fated A.B.D.A. Fleet was reduced to two ships, the rest being either sunk or put out of commission, the *Houston* together with *Perth* made a desperate dash to Sunda Strait again in an effort to escape. But along with the *Perth*, in the early hours of 1 March 1942, and after a fierce engagement with the Japanese fleet supporting the troop landings in Banten Bay, the U.S.S. *Houston* was sunk off St Nicolas Point, West Java. Captain Rooks, and some five hundred of the ship's company died with her.

At the conclusion of this brief outline of the American cruiser's history, the headman told me that when the battle of Sunda Strait started, his people had fled up the mountainside behind the village, and from their vantage point overlooking the bay had witnessed the entire action.

From what he said the Allied cruisers never stood a chance. Surrounded and out-gunned by the enemy, they were hit with torpedo attacks from destroyers, pounded by cruisers, and bombed by aircraft. In the illumination provided by the enemy searchlights, the Bantenese could see the planes diving again and again, with the tracer bullets bouncing off the decks of the two ships as they were raked with shell and machine-gun fire.

In the morning following the battle, the headman said that some of the survivors from our ships were actually swept by the currents into Banten Bay with the invading forces, and although the survivors were unarmed, with many badly wounded, the Japanese had butchered them with their Samurai swords as they staggered exhausted on to the beach. He didn't know if the sailors were Australian or American, but later when the Japanese had moved inland, his people came down from the mountain and buried the bodies in graves they dug in the sand.

Out to sea, the masts of a large ship could be seen protruding from the water. The ship was there for a long time, and none of the Bantenese was allowed to go near it. One day some more Japanese came. They were in what must have been fully equipped diving vessels, for after working on the wreck for some months, they finally finished cutting it up, and took it away.

From this and other information received I evolved a theory on the fate of the *Houston*. I consider that it was she who was salvaged by the Japanese during their occupation of Java in 1942-45. I must emphasise that it is only a theory, based on the known facts, and some supposition on my part.

It is generally accepted that the *Houston* sank closer in-shore than the *Perth*, and although the level of the bed of the Java Sea is patchy, with the recorded soundings showing current-scoured hollows of up to fifty fathoms in depth, it would seem the *Houston* sank in only twenty fathoms. Being a 10,000-ton heavy cruiser, sinking upright in this depth, would leave the tops of her masts well clear of the surface.

It is also known that the damage caused by *Perth* and *Houston* to the invasion fleet led the Japanese to think one of them must have been a battleship, as the Japanese wouldn't believe that two cruisers could put up such a fight. If the Japanese thought the *Houston* was a battleship, which represented a very valuable prize in non-ferrous metal, it is easy to understand their interest in what would be to them an easy salvage job.

Also it is not hard to believe that when the *Houston*'s bell was recovered by the divers, one of the Japanese

107

officers decided to keep it, and in due course, and by who knows what means, the magnificently engraved bell ended up in Manila. That it should be a showpiece there in a private museum, where it was reported to have been sighted after the war, is also logical.

I wrote to Walter Allen, my friend in Houston, Texas, outlining my theory, and he made further inquiries through the *Houston Post*. The information the *Post* uncovered was startling. Apparently when President Johnson visited Corregidor in 1966, President Marcos of the Philippines presented him with the bell of the *Houston*. This was then loaded aboard the President's plane, flown directly to Washington, and placed in the Presidential archives, where it has been ever since.

President Johnson's press secretary, Mr Christian, advised the *Post* that the bell, which bears the inscription "U.S.S. *Houston*, 1930," has an additional inscription of:

"This bell of the U.S.S. *Houston*, United States Pacific Fleet, sunk during the battle of the Java Sea during World War II, was recovered by the Republic of the Philippines. It was presented to Lyndon B. Johnson, President of the United States of America, by President Ferdinand Marcos of the Republic of the Philippines at Batong Buhay, Corregidor 26th October, 1966."

Mr Christian said that President Johnson was unaware of how the Philippine Republic had gained possession of the bell, and as President Marcos made no explanation it seems he didn't know either. But I think that this last relic of the mighty *Houston*, the 'Galloping Ghost of the China Sea', was carried to Manila in a Japanese diving officer's baggage, marked 'spoils of war'.

Perhaps this unknown diver was also a lover of ships, and couldn't bring himself to allow this priceless artefact to be melted down for scrap. If the assumption is correct and he had some feeling for the ship and her crew, as a fellow-diver I would salute him.

108

Sharks and Souvenirs

DURING THE THIRTY DIVES I MADE ON THE "PERTH" we recovered some twenty-four different relics. These included shell cases from the four-inch gun turrets, navigational instruments, and a signalling light from the bridge, voice tubes and gyro repeaters from the wheelhouse, and other miscellaneous pieces from different areas.

Some came easily, and these I was mostly able to carry up with me. Some were more difficult to recover. The signalling light from the bridge probably caused us the most trouble. I had seen it on several occasions; it was about the size of a twelve-and-a-half gallon drum, and looked as if it would be heavy and awkward to handle.

Lying half out of its mounts with one of its octagonal panes of glass broken, the light also had a large hole in its side, indicating that it had been hit by shell fire. It took a whole dive to clear it completely from the ship, and the next day when I dived again, I took down an inch-thick manila rope that Sumantri had brought back with him from Djakarta. The rope was stiff and difficult to tie, but when it was secure I gave the four-pulls signal, indicating to the boys up in the dinghy that it was time to heave.

For the next five minutes we staged a tug of war with the light, and as the men in the dinghy pulled, I pushed, but it wouldn't budge. Panting with the exertion I gave the two-pull stand-by signal and backed off. I couldn't work it out as I felt sure the light was free of its gimbals, but something was holding it. Swimming down under the mounting, I searched around carefully, and after a minute or so found the trouble. There was an electric cable still feeding into the light. The cable was as thick as my thumb and as strong as a hawser, and looking at it I knew we wouldn't be raising the light that dive, for it was definitely a hacksaw job.

Later, with the bluntest hacksaw in Indonesia, I finally succeeded in cutting the cable. This time, after the signal to pull was given, the light rose majestically from out of its gimbals, and in fits and starts as the chaps pulled, it started its long journey to the surface. I was just about to turn away, satisfied that the light was as good as recovered, when it suddenly slipped lengthways out of the holding noose, catching at the last second on one of the signalman's shoulder rests.

Pushing off the ship I chased up after it, and taking hold of the rope frantically gave the stand-by signal. But as the boys kept pulling, I realised that the rope had so much weight on it the signal couldn't be felt, and at every jerk the light threatened to slip clean out of the noose. Looking down I couldn't see the ship; it was already lost in the grey fog below, so I had no option but to ride the rope up, for if I stayed with the rope there was a chance I could hold it on to the light, but if I left it the light was sure to be lost.

Telling myself I probably wouldn't be able to find the ship again anyway, I wrapped my leg round the light and

110

placing one arm through the noose, held on to the shoulder rest with my free hand, thus keeping the rope from slipping off.

It was a slow, agonising trip. Every now and again the pull would stop, and the light and I, welded together in our silent death-like embrace, would spin slowly round at the end of the rope. As the frequency of these pauses increased in number, I couldn't help smiling at the thought of the boys in the dinghy, for with my weight to lift as well as the heavy light it must have been tough going. By the time we reached the surface I think everyone was exhausted, but if John and Sumantri hadn't jumped overboard, and taken the strain, we still could have lost it. All I could do after two of the leading seamen, Pati and Johnno, had hauled me aboard was to lie gasping in the bilge, unable even to raise my hand to take off my mask. Scammell, who works on the principle that if you yell loud enough non-English-speaking people will understand you, was going great guns. But eventually he and Sumantri made the rope more secure, and after a mammoth effort and a couple of near misses they wrestled the light up on to the deck of the *Aries*.

The four-inch shell cases, while heavy enough, didn't present anywhere near the problem of the signal light. They were mostly recovered from S2, the starboard aft turret, about forty feet up from the sea-bed.

The first time I looked inside I could see a number of empty shell cases and several live rounds in a heap on the deck. Two of the live rounds were bent at right angles, again the evidence of a direct hit.

Thinking that Gordon Reid would like a shellcase, as he had been a four-inch gunner, I moved in to pick one up, only to find that they were all fused together with calcified marine growth. However, as I had my pick hammer with me I sat down in the turret and started the delicate job of chipping the shells apart. I knew it was highly unlikely that one of the live rounds would explode, although it did cross my mind, and after banging away for a while a spent shell broke free. Taking it in my arms I crawled out of the turret on my elbows, intending to place the shellcase in the rice sack tied outside.

The rice sack was a new idea we had evolved for the recovery of light weight objects, and now I took it with me on every dive. It was attached to about ninety metres of special steel core sounding line, and at the conclusion of the dive it would be hauled back to the surface.

Clearing the entrance to the turret, I scrambled for a footing, trying to stand up and at the same time reaching for the bag, but the unaccustomed weight threw me off balance and hugging the shellcase I plummeted down the canted gun deck to the sea bed. Kneeling in the sand beside the huge bulk of the ship, I juggled the shellcase into a better position, and then pushed off in an attempt to swim back up the forty feet. But I was like a fledgling that had fallen out of its nest, and after a couple of pathetic attempts, decided that it would be much easier to bring the sack down to the shell. This I did, and after some trouble pushing the spiky shell into the bag, gave the signal to haul away.

As I watched the bag starting its ascent, it occurred to me that there was something wrong with the angle of the rope—it was too perpendicular for the way the current was running. Looking up, I could see why. The rope had fouled over a spar on the aft control, and if the sack with the heavy shell hit the spar it would more than likely be torn off.

Shoving off from the sea bed, I began a frantic race to the spar with the jerking sack. Just making it to the obstruction first, I straddled it, and leaning down managed to heave the shell over. But as the bag scraped across, it caught the quick-release buckle of my weight belt and this item, correctly doing its job, immediately released itself. My first knowledge that the belt had gone was when I sat up thankfully on the spar to watch the sack disappear upwards, only to see to my dismay the weights going up with it. Once more I had to sprint after the bag, and after catching up with it and retrieving the belt, I sank wearily back onto the ship. By now the current had carried me back past the quarterdeck, and rather grimly I started the long pull up-current to the number three buoy rope on the four-inch gun deck.

After I'd gone about half way, I stopped for a rest by bracing myself against a stanchion. Hanging there for a few seconds I realised I was cutting it fine, for I was nearly out of air. Glancing up I couldn't help the sudden wave of fear that swept through me, for there, like a group of larrikins waiting at a street corner, was the shark pack . . .

Lately when we'd met I'd noticed that the sharks were becoming more aggressive and I'd decided to give them as wide a berth as possible. But today it seemed I had no option, for the pack was between me and the shot line, and as I was nearly out of air there was no time to skirt round them or to drop back down current to the number four buoy cable aft. Consequently I had no alternative but to go through the sharks, and be quick about it at that.

Taking a firm grip on the stubby handle of the pick hammer and trying not to think about what would happen if they really got dinkum, I swam on up the deck and moved into the circling pack.

The sharks were about nine or ten feet long, somewhat smaller than the ones we encounter back in Australia, but lean and fast. By now they had become agitated and that didn't help matters. Almost immediately they started making their characteristic passing runs, like fighter planes strafing a bomber . . . coming in close but never quite making contact . . . and for a while they had me pinned down on the deck.

I was worried about my air and the fact that I wasn't getting any closer to the shot line, but for the moment I couldn't move, for without the protection of the deck I could have been in trouble.

113

When the sharks came in too close I swiped at them with the pick hammer, and hit one a glancing blow on the nose before he turned away. It was probably the best thing that could have happened for it seemed to discourage them temporarily and they kept their distance, which allowed me to make a dash over the open water separating me from the four-inch gun deck.

But the sharks soon resumed their game, and I remember glancing longingly into the first of the four-inch turrets as I passed for it offered a secure sanctuary, but by now my air gauge was showing a virtual nil reading and I had to keep going.

Finally I reached the shot line and shakily stood up, pausing for a moment to wave my arm at them in what I hopefully imagined would be taken for an act of defiance.

It was all show, and probably fooled the sharks least of all because, as my hand was trembling so much, in the midst of the gesture I nearly dropped the bloody hammer.

But it wasn't over yet, for the trip back to the surface was a nightmare as the sharks followed me up, making their sporadic torpedo-like passes from out of the grey fog.

About halfway they suddenly stopped, as if by some pre-arranged agreement among themselves, but at the time I was unaware of the arrangement and the next eighty feet or so of ascent I think was worse, as I looked in all directions at once waiting for them to reappear.

There were odd days when I didn't see the sharks at all, but mostly we would play hide and seek at some time during my dives on the ship. Among my gear on the *Aries* was a heavy speargun fitted with a .303 power head, or "smokey" as we call them, and while this would have tickled them up, I was usually so burdened with ropes and other items that I couldn't carry the gun. Instead I tried to condition myself mentally to ignore the sharks, and to some extent was successful, although their sudden appearance always gave me a fright.

It was the times they were on the surface before a dive

that I disliked them most, for it would be difficult to imagine anything more sinister than the sight of their black dorsal fins cutting through the water as they lazily glided round the buoys. This was also perhaps the time of the greatest danger, that of entering the water and swimming down to the ship, and I remember cursing them, as the long hard haul was bad enough on its own, without worrying about the sharks. But although they came very close, they never actually attacked, and I did learn to live with them after a fashion.

In contrast to my feelings against the sharks were my feelings in favour of the groper, and in no time I had groper friends all over the ship. They seemed to stick to their own particular area, as I always saw the same ones in the same places. Huge creatures, and insatiably curious, the gropers' sluggish movements give the impression that they are a bit dim-witted, and it was obvious that my sudden appearance in their lives was the greatest event that had happened in years.

Dopey, the one I got to know best, lived on the bridge, and as I worked away at recovering different items I could always rely on him to be looking over my shoulder. One day as I was carefully removing a voice tube mouthpiece, he became so attracted to the white cotton bands round the wrists of my gloves that, coming right in, he started to try to eat them. Without looking up from what I was doing I pulled the glove away, and gave him a smart back hander on the nose. It was only after making contact that I realised what I'd done, for Dopey, all 300 pounds of him, could have bitten my hand off at the armpit. Looking quickly around to see how he'd taken it, I saw that he'd backed off, the great sad face registering his deep hurt at so unkind a cut. After a while he forgave me and once more came in to peer over my shoulder, but I noticed that he didn't attempt to bite the glove again.

There were many other creatures who had made the *Perth* their home. The dozens of green turtles, some

115

weighing over 200 pounds, the hundreds of varieties of fish, the many different rays and something else, whose identity I never established, but which was so large that it completely blocked out the meagre light from above. It wasn't Dopey, as out of the corner of my eye I could see him alongside me. But as I was busy at the time I didn't look up, and it was only later after it had gone that I started to wonder what had been poised above. It was probably just as well I never found out.

From inside the wheelhouse I recovered a beautiful copper voice tube mouthpiece on the inside of which was an engraved brass plate reading "No. 44. Upper Bridge Starboard". Also in the wheelhouse was a bronze gyro compass repeater, and as it was extremely heavy, I cradled it in one arm and laboriously climbed up the front of the bridge to where I'd left the sounding line and the rice sack. Placing the repeater and mouthpiece in the bag, I swam across the corner of the bridge to where shell fire had partly exposed the wheelhouse below. Holding on to the deck, I lay still and peered through the hole, but the visibility was under two feet, and deciding that I wouldn't find anything that way, started to push back out of the wreckage. As I did so something under my hand moved slightly, and looking down I could see a round metal object about the size and shape of a "hard hat" diver's helmet.

Dusting the silt away with my hand I uncovered two glass windows near the top and realised what I'd found: it was the ship's compass.

It was an exciting find, and I carefully prised it out of the damaged corner. When the compass came free its weight surprised me, and like the time with the four-inch shellcase, I took off.

Sliding and crashing down the almost vertical deck I ended up in a heap on the port side. Appreciating that it was far too dangerous a manoeuvre for this depth, I berated myself for not being more careful, for not only had my mask been knocked off but the demand valve, supplying

116

me with air from the cylinder, had nearly been pulled from my mouth. Fortunately the mask was still stuck on the top of my head, and quickly putting it back on, I cleared it of water, for without the mask I was blind and would have had a difficult job finding my way back to the shot line.

However, I still had the compass, and placing it carefully down on the deck I swam back up to where I'd tied the sounding line. I nearly untied the sack containing the repeater, but as the line had a steel core I felt it would easily hold the extra weight. Once down on the port side again, I securely lashed the compass above the bag, and when completely satisfied that it was all right, I gave the signal to pull it up. Watching until the rice sack had disappeared into the fog I swam up to the number two buoy cable attached to the bridge, and as fast as I could followed it back to the surface.

I knew the sounding line had broken and that we'd lost the compass as soon as I saw John's face. Holding on to the side of the dinghy, for a moment I was inconsolable. This was too much.

Vaguely I heard poor old Scammell trying to explain what had happened. "I felt the line start to stretch," he said, "and I stopped the haul. Then as we were over half way to the surface, I reckoned it should be okay and we started again, but at about sixty feet the rope snapped like a carrot. What did you have on it? Was it something valuable?"

Jerking my head up I glared at him over the side of the dinghy. "Have we brought anything up yet that hasn't been valuable?" I snarled. "It was only the bloody compass, do you call that valuable?"

I was being unfair and I knew it. John was as concerned about every aspect of the venture as I was, and it wasn't his fault that the ropes were all rotten. But I was so put out at the loss that I could have howled, and he was the only one handy I could sound off at.

That afternoon we tied the inch manila rope to a fifty-six-pound weight and dropped it over the bow of the dinghy,

117

which was again being held to number two buoy. My theory was that the weight should land on the sea bed at approximately the same spot as the compass. If, when I reached the bottom, I couldn't see the compass I intended making circular searches using the weight as a datum point.

Circular searching is the accepted procedure when operating in water of poor visibility. A rope is tied to the weight, and the diver backs off until the weight is just visible. He then completes a 360-degree sweep and if the object for which he is looking is between him and the weight he naturally sees it. If it is not, the diver marks the rope by tying a piece of white rag to it, and retreating again until this is only just visible he completes another sweep. If the visibility is zero, basically the same procedure is followed, but it is all done by feel. As soon as I started down the rope I could feel the weight come off the bottom, and by the time I reached it the force of the current had the weight streaming six feet off the sea bed. After a struggle I forced it down on to the sand, and as my time at this depth was short, I quickly tied the piece of sounding line that I'd brought with me to the weight, and began the search.

Crawling against the current reminded me of Scott of the Antarctic in a blizzard. Going with the current I was like a tumble weed in a desert gale. After one and a half sweeps I was completely exhausted, and realised that the circular searches were beyond me. In sheer desperation I paid myself out down current to the full extent of the line, hoping to find the compass by chance, but there was nothing.

We were a quiet ship's company on the way back to Merak. I was having a bit of a sulk, John was busy preparing something special for tea in an effort to cheer me up, and the boys had suddenly revived their lagging interest in chipping sponge and other growth off the signal light. After half and hour or so I stopped feeling sorry for myself, and started to try to plan for another go at recovering the compass.

118

The best way I could think of was to take one end of the manila rope down with me, and then after reaching the spot where I'd sent up the compass, I'd leave the ship and strike out down current, following the course the compass took before the sounding line broke. If I didn't find anything I could give the haul away signal, and the boys would pull me up.

Next morning with this plan in mind I again dived down the number two buoy cable. Looped over my shoulder was my end of the heavy rope, and so as not to foul it on the ship, when nearly there I pushed off the buoy cable and swam clean over her, landing on the sea bed at the port side of the bridge.

Wasting no time, I took my bearings and pushed off down current. In seconds the *Perth* had disappeared and I felt very much on my own, but also within seconds I saw the rice sack and the compass. They were dead ahead and I was coming down on them as if directed by radar. From then on their recovery was just a matter of routine, and after triple-tying the rope I gave the signal, and we were all pulled to the surface.

Back on the *Aries* we inspected the relics and found that what we'd recovered was not the compass, but the compass housing or binnacle. Apparently the compass itself had been blown clean out of the housing, but its gimbal ring, with the name "Sperry" stamped on it, was still inside along with the auxiliary batteries.

It didn't really matter, the binnacle was a beautiful piece, and I carefully cleaned the sponge and coral from it. In my mind I could see the binnacle in its glass case at the Canberra War Memorial, and it was with somewhat of a shock that I realised our job was nearly done, and that we could start thinking about going home.

Remembrance

THERE WERE STILL TWO IMPORTANT FUNCTIONS LEFT TO carry out. One was to photograph the *Perth*, and the other was to hold a wreath-laying ceremony. While many such services had been held by passing British ships over the years, they had been many miles off her actual bearings, and we considered that this was a wonderful opportunity to hold a service right over the ship.

I had already obtained the necessary permission from the Indonesian Navy, and had arranged with Freddie Sherborne to come down from Djakarta with a wreath. At seven o'clock in the morning of the Sunday we had chosen for the ceremony, Freddie, Bobbie, and young Kristen, arrived in Merak in the Embassy Landrover, and after they had been piped aboard, we cast off and moved up the Strait. Out at the diving area I had removed all the buoys from the ship, bar number four, the one secured to the quarterdeck, and after lining everyone up along the starboard side of the

TOP: With the ship's company at the salute, Bobby and Christen Sherborne drop the wreath over the side. BOTTOM: As though drawn by a magnet, the wreath floated to the buoy still moored to the *Perth*'s quarterdeck

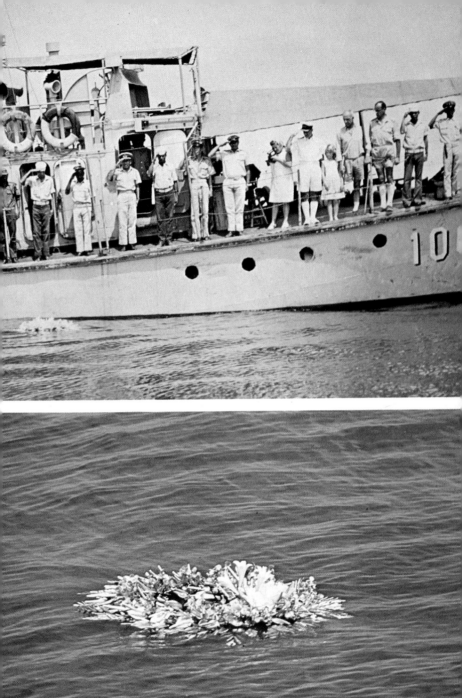

Aries we steamed slowly past the buoy, our object being to lay the wreath up current and let it float back as close to the buoy as possible.

With the crew at the salute, Bobbie and Kristen dropped the wreath over the side, and it was then that a very strange thing happened. The current, which had run a banker for the whole of the three weeks we had been diving, suddenly stopped, and the wreath as if drawn by a magnet slowly drifted towards the buoy and hung there, not three feet off it, for nearly twenty minutes. Any other day it would have been whipped away in seconds.

On the last two dives, the twenty-ninth and thirtieth, I photographed the ship. Working from the shot line on the quarter deck I took flash shots of the Gorgonia coral on the bridge, the guns, the torpedo tubes, the quarterdeck itself, and frightened hell out of poor old Dopey with a close up shot that I snapped of his head.

It was towards the end of the twenty-ninth dive that I got into trouble. I'd polished up some of the brass work on the torpedo tubes and was just bringing them into focus with the camera, when something grabbed me by the back of the neck. It was as if I were nailed to a wall, for I couldn't move. Overcoming the desire to struggle, I cautiously felt around behind my head. At first there was nothing. Then I found the tangle of wire that had fouled tight round the Scuba regulator.

This wasn't the best place to be caught, for the Scuba regulator is only attached to the cylinder by a finger-tight fitting on to an "O" ring seal, and any sudden movement could dislodge it. If this happened I'd be without air. Checking the high pressure gauge I estimated that there was only enough air for another five minutes. I'd have to act quickly, and as struggling was out of the question I decided to take the Scuba off and untangle the wire when I could see it.

This normally wouldn't have been so difficult but the current and all the extra gear I had on slowed me down.

Top: The buoy moored to the *Perth*'s quarterdeck. Bottom: Mrs H. Waller, widow of the captain of the first H.M.A.S. *Perth*, lays another wreath during Remembrance Day ceremonies at the Australian War Memorial, Canberra. Admiral Sir Allan McNicol, R.A.N., Chief of Naval Staff, stands behind her

First I had to get rid of the plastic airways bag, containing the flash bulbs, that was floating above my head as the thin handles of the bag were twisted round the neck strap of the camera, which also had to be removed. It was a fiddly job, with everything having to be done either behind or above my head, and it was aggravated by my mask and snorkel getting in the way and my rising consternation at the feeling I wasn't getting anywhere.

When I finally succeeded in removing the bag and camera I had nowhere to put them. Being suspended off the ship as I was, and not wanting to lose the expensive camera, and much more important, the film it contained, I wasted precious time desperately looking for somewhere safe to drop it. But as I couldn't see anywhere suitable in my limited range of vision, I let the bag go and hung the camera strap over my foot. Next came the weight belt. This I also draped over my foot, and then I undid the Scuba harness. Slipping out of it I gently turned round, and with the demand valve still in my mouth untangled the wire.

A glance at my watch and a quick check of the air pressure showed about two minutes' time left. I'd made it . . .

That afternoon I dived to the *Perth* for the last time. First I finished taking the photographs and when this was done I made my way up to the bridge to hold a small service of my own. I'd discussed it with John the night before, and we had already chosen the prayer. Originally we intended it for the boys of the *Perth* and *Houston* but I decided at the last minute to include the chaps on the Japanese trooper.

Crouching down out of the current behind the bridge screen, with the Gorgonia spray for an altar and my friend the groper, who had taken up his accustomed place beside me, standing in as witness, I said the familiar words:

> Our Father, which art in Heaven
> Hallowed be Thy name
> Thy kingdom come
> Thy will be done . . .

122

Good-bye, Daddy

A T THE CONCLUSION OF THE DIVING WE RECOVERED THE number four buoy cable and immediately sailed for Djakarta, arriving at Priok late that night.

About the first thing John and I did, after transferring our gear from the *Aries* to the *Bergamahl*, was to have a bath, or more correctly an Indonesian version of one. The Indonesian bathroom is about the size of a shower alcove, and in one corner is a type of wash trough full of water and a dipper. The bather, standing in the middle, pours water over himself with the dipper; once you become accustomed to it the system is most effective.

In the morning, we supervised the transfer of the *Perth* relics from the *Aries* to the Yacht Club wharf, where they were picked up by a truck and taken to the Hydrographic Command. John and I followed along in Sumantri's jeep.

Waiting in Commodore Wardiman's office were about a dozen reporters and journalists. While giving them a run-down on the trip I mentioned to the Commodore that I would like the crew of the *Aries* to become members of the Underwater Explorers Club, adding that perhaps he would give them official permission to wear the U.E.C. silver diver badge as part of their uniform.

The Commodore promised he would consider it, and subsequently the certificates and badges were presented to the crew at an official investiture parade after I'd left for home. But apparently one of the reporters must have misunderstood me, for it was later stated in the Djakarta press that the Australian Government had struck a special medal in appreciation of the help given by the Indonesian Navy. Commodore Wardiman of course knew this was not correct, but I think for my sake he never denied it. Also, as he was pro-Australian, and like so many Indonesians a natural born diplomat, he probably thought it represented good public relations for both countries anyway.

The next step was to transport the relics home to Australia. There were two alternatives. One was shipping them back, but when we checked the departures from Priok the only vessel leaving in the foreseeable future was sailing to Hong Kong. She could have taken them, but if the relics went this way they would have to be transhipped in China.

"Not on your life," I said to Freddie. "That's no good, hell we may never see them again."

He agreed, and we decided to have a go at asking Qantas to fly them home. The manager of Qantas, a golfing friend of Freddie's, told us that the decision to fly the 600 pounds of relics to Australia, on a no cost basis, was beyond his authority, but he promised to send a cable to Canberra and see what he could do. This was a blow as we reckoned it would take the best part of a week to receive a reply, and it meant that I would have to hang around Djakarta waiting. But although I had to wait, John didn't, and as he still had ten days or so up his sleeve before meeting his wife Nancy in Singapore, he decided to spend the time in Bali.

I'd have liked to have gone with him, but I couldn't leave

124

Djakarta until the problem of the relics had been solved, so next day Sumantri and I put him on the train for Surabaya, and laden down with his cameras, faithful old Scammell left me.

As Freddie had invited me to stay at his house for the remainder of my time in Djakarta, we transferred my gear from the *Bergamahl*, and for the next few days, while I waited for news from Qantas, the Sherbornes gave me a great time.

With Bobbie and Kristen I went for a drive up into the mountains where we visited the tea plantations, and bought watercolour paintings and other souvenirs from the wayside peddlers. I also helped them shop in the markets in Djakarta, and bought a couple of colourful shirts at the Batik factory. One night we went to a party at the Indian Embassy, and another evening they asked Sumantri and his attractive wife over for dinner.

After about five days Freddie rang from his office at the Embassy. He had bad news. The Qantas manager had called, and my request to have the relics flown back to Australia had been turned down. He was as upset as I was, and had pointed out to the Qantas chap that the relics were not mine, but that they belonged to Australia, and he thought it was a pretty poor show. Although the airways official was sympathetic there was nothing he could do.

There was now only one thing left. I decided to get help from Geoff Giles or Bert Kelly after I'd returned home and therefore arranged to have the relics crated and left in Freddie's care at the Embassy.

The night before I left Java, Jim Carr, the American Assistant Naval Attaché, invited me over for dinner. During the evening, the subject of divers having a predominance of daughters in their children came up. Someone in the group asked me if I had children and I replied that I had four, adding that they were all daughters. "Really, is that so?" a woman exclaimed. "Tell me, were you active when your wife conceived?"

125

Another guest there was an Indonesian underwater salvage contractor, who was keen for me to dive on a ship that had been torpedoed in the Bali Strait. The ship was reported to have a million dollars worth of tin in her holds, but she was deep, about 300 feet. For a moment or two I considered having a go, but declined for I'd had enough, and I wanted to get the relics home.

Actually I was more interested at the time in pinching one of Jim Carr's naval caps, as I was forming a collection of the three countries, Australia, America, and Indonesia, that were involved in the Sunda Strait diving. I had already won caps off both Freddie and Sumantri and Jim was the object of my next attack.

By the time the evening was over I thought he had forgotten about it, but just as I was leaving he slipped upstairs and came back with one of his U.S. Navy caps. It completed the trio.

One morning Sumantri and I were browsing round a small antique shop in a back street in Djakarta when the proprietor, a wizened up little Indonesian, shyly asked me if I was the Australian who had been diving on the *Perth*.

When I told him I was he said he had only met one other Australian, and added that he was the bravest man he ever knew.

It was during the war in 1943 at Bandung, in Japanese-occupied Central West Java. The Australian, Lieutenant-Colonel Douglas Smith, had worked in the hotel that the Indonesians ran, disguised as an Armenian cook.

"Smithy," as he was called, taught them to play whist, and during the six months he was with the Indonesians told them stories about his home town, Coolangatta, of the surf and beaches, and of life in Australia. Every night, despite their repeated warnings, he would slip out of the hotel, never saying why or where he was going. They all knew it was just a matter of time before he was caught, and eventually one night the Japanese were waiting as he tried to creep back in.

The Indonesian said that for some days "Smithy" was tortured, until finally, no doubt realising that his position was hopeless, he confessed to having sent messages by radio to the Americans.

The Japanese gave him a trial and then executed him by hanging. Placing his hand on his skinny chest, the Indonesian, almost in tears at the memory of it, concluded sadly, "At the time of the execution, we were all quiet here in our hearts."

Freddie just dropped me off at the airport. There was no point in him waiting, for the plane's departure could take hours. After clearing Customs I sat down on one of the hard seats in the waiting area, and almost immediately a scruffy-looking character came up trying to put over some sort of deal.

I was preoccupied and wasn't really listening, but after a while I glanced up and said, "Buzz off, old chap, or I'll have you arrested. You may not know it, but I have friends in high places."

The Indonesian, who had no idea of what I was talking about, persisted and I realised he wanted a cigarette. With a sigh I searched through my brief case, and handed over my last packet of Rothmans.

As he ambled off one of my "friends in high places" sat down next to me.

We had already said our goodbyes the day before, but apparently they weren't enough, for hunching forward on the seat and staring at his hands he said, without even looking at me, "Hullo Daddy, they tell me you don't live here anymore."

The Japanese are an odd bunch. In the 1930s they were rated as cheap copyists of other peoples' brains and initiative, while during the war they earned for themselves the reputation of being dirty and brutal and something less than sub-human.

Consequently it was interesting to observe the crew on the Japan Airlines flight from Djakarta to Singapore, as the hostesses with their delicate beauty and thoughtful attentive service were a far cry from the impressions left by the Knights of the Bushido.

One realised of course that the girls hadn't been picked for the job because they resembled Phyllis Diller made up for her act, but nevertheless they were surprising and it was difficult not to respond to their polite friendliness.

Problems solved

THE DAY AFTER ARRIVING HOME I WAS SITTING AT MY
desk in the office, staring morosely at the pile of
work that had built up.

I'd just returned from the *Advertiser* building, the home
of our morning paper, where I'd asked the chaps in the
photographic section to develop the underwater film in my
camera.

To their sympathetic dismay and my horror the exposed
film showed a complete blank, not even a smudge. Somehow John and I had loaded the camera incorrectly. It was
about the last straw, and I was fed up, but still had to face
the job of bringing the relics back. Just then the phone rang.
It was Perth, Western Australia, calling. "Peter Finn, Chief
of Staff *Sunday Times*, speaking," the voice said. "What's
this about your having trouble flying the *Perth* relics back
to Australia?" I told him the trouble. "Okay," he said,
"leave it with me. I'll ring you back in a couple of hours."

By the time Finn rang back he had the return of the relics all arranged, but he stipulated two conditions. The *Sunday Times*, in conjunction with Malayan Singapore Airlines and Channel 9 in Perth, would fly the relics home if I'd present a part of the ship to the City of Perth, and secondly I had to come over as their guest, and be there when the relics arrived. "Boy," I said, as the weight of the responsibility of it all slid off me, "you've got a deal."

There was a large crowd at the Adelaide airport the day my wife and I took off for Perth. I thought it was pretty decent of them all to come down and see us off, until my wife pointed out that we were on the same plane as the South Australian football team, which was also on its way to Perth.

I'd already flown over once since the return from Indonesia, when along with twenty or so of the *Perth* survivors I'd met the M.S.A. plane from Djakarta carrying the relics. They had travelled well, and after we had inspected them the President of the *Perth* Association, Charlie Thompson, agreed to their being displayed in the foyer of the Rural and Industries Bank. Later I was told that during the five days the relics were on display over 10,000 Western Australians came in to see them.

We decided on one of the four-inch shell cases as a gift to the City. As it needed to be properly mounted I said I'd take it home to Adelaide, and when it was ready send it back. But they wouldn't hear of it. "You can't just send it back," Arthur Bancroft, one of the survivors, said. "The agreement was that you present it to the Lord Mayor yourself."

When the shell had been cut in halves and suitably mounted, I rang the Adelaide T.A.A. Manager, Reg Rechner, and thanked him for the proposed free trip. "It's no trouble," he said. "Perhaps your wife would like to go as well." I assured him she would, and it was settled.

The Lord Mayor of Perth, Mr Veryard, received the shell case at a reception in the Civic Centre, and afterwards it was permanently fixed on the wall above his desk. On each side of it hang the two Naval caps that I also gave to the City, one is Australian and the other American. The Indonesian cap I kept for myself, as I considered that, like the character who gave it to me, it was my own personal property.

The other half of the shell case that now hangs in the Perth Civic Centre I also had mounted, and later in Canberra gave it to the American Ambassador to Australia, Mr Ed. Clarke, with the request that it be sent on to the City of Houston in Texas, the thought being that as I couldn't find their ship, the people of Houston may appreciate part of the *Perth*. In due course Mayor Louie Welch of Houston wrote thanking me for the shell and advised me that it was now a permanent part of his office. Although it was not really planned that the two halves of the shell should find homes so many thousands of miles apart, one couldn't wish for a more appropriate ending.

After they left Perth, the relics made a tour of the different State Capitals, as it was considered that before they reached their permanent home in Canberra, survivors in each State should have a chance to see them.

Again Reg Rechner and T.A.A. came to our aid, and they flew both the relics and me to Brisbane, Sydney, and Melbourne. It was time-consuming and a bit costly but I considered it was well worth the trouble, for in each city the relics received the same reception from the survivors. It always moved me to see the way these men, whether it be the Ern Tooveys in Queensland, the Max Jaggers in New South Wales, the Andy Mitchells in South Australia, or the Ray Parkins in Victoria, reacted to seeing part of their ship again.

Not all the relics made it to Canberra, for soon after the gift was made of the four-inch shell case to the City of Perth, requests for mementoes of the ship came thick and fast. The requests were all worthy and I had a difficult time deciding who should receive the limited number of items that were available.

131

A porthole rim went to the *Perth* Memorial Hall at the R.A.N. shore-base in Fremantle, and the Ex-Navalmen's Association at Elizabeth in South Australia has part of a navigational instrument from the bridge.

One of the other shell cases was cut in halves, and after the two sections were mounted, one was given to Gordon Reid and the other to John Scammell. I offered the Captain of the new H.M.A.S. *Perth* a voice tube mouthpiece, and after the Naval Board approved its acceptance, part of the old ship officially became part of the new one.

On the wall at Naval Memorial House in North Adelaide there is an engraved brass plate from the engine room telegraph system, and the different *Perth* Associations in each State all have their own special pieces.

During the transportation of the relics from one State to another the signalman's shoulder-rest from the starboard bridge light broke off, and as the light was "Buzzer" Bee's action station the night the ship was sunk, I sent the broken shoulder-rest over to him in Perth.

Here and there are some other pieces, like the brass bolt in the foyer of the Rural and Industries Bank, the copper container from the wheelhouse that Ray Parkin now has in his study, and the voice tube mouthpiece on the wall in my office, and although all these relics are appreciated to the full, I think the one that is perhaps cherished the most is the lampholder from the binnacle.

Made of brass, it originally held the light that lit the compass at night. It was a wonder that the frail welds securing the lampholder to the binnacle held on as long as they did, but shortly after it arrived home the solder became brittle and it broke away.

When I gave the lampholder to Mrs Waller I told her that it came from the bridge, and that Captain Waller must have been standing close to it when he died. Now every year, on Christmas Eve, she places a lighted candle in it, the burning flame being a silent tribute to the memory of her husband, his ship, and his men.

132

Final Ceremony

ON REMEMBRANCE DAY THE CHIEF OF NAVAL STAFF, Admiral Sir Alan McNicol, received the relics of the *Perth* on behalf of the Royal Australian Navy and the Australian War Memorial. There was quite a large audience packed into the Naval Gallery, and as I listened to the speeches I glanced across at the painting of Hec Waller, remembering that other time, when I'd first stood in front of it, and although the occasion had been only a few months before, in some ways it seemed a lifetime. As my thoughts drifted back over the period I couldn't help realising how lucky I'd been, for while it can be argued that what is frequently termed a "lucky break" is not really luck at all but more often is the result of sheer persistence, I still did get the breaks.

That we worked hard, and also that between us we had our certain abilities, was incidental, for these things are the normal prerequisites, the basic requirements, without which no one should attempt such a project. But it is an accepted fact that in many fields of endeavour there is a very fine line between success and failure, and this cannot always be determined by the degree of ability or effort. You still have to get the breaks, and you have to get them at the right time.

There was no doubt that my breaks had come with the people I'd involved, the first being the day I said Jim Forbes was my friend, for this alone must have helped me more times than I ever knew.

Then there was General Kosasih, whose initial encouragement and advice showed me how to plan it all, and Commodore Wardiman who, in spite of the considered opinions of his fellow officers, and who no doubt at times had a few qualms of his own, still continued to back me when nearly everyone else had baled out.

What would I have done without the support of old friends like John Scammell and Geoff Giles, and that of the new ones such as Freddie Sherborne, Sumantri, the Bantenese fishermen, and the crew of the *Aries*? As I sat musing over the long list my eyes drifted back again to the painting of Hec Walker, and looking at it I knew he'd have understood, for he would have known the value of people and the value of getting the breaks.

I heard someone mention my name and with a start realised it was nearly time to make my speech. Looking into the sea of faces I picked out my wife and children and smiled at the sight of our four girls, sitting proudly bolt upright, on their best behaviour.

I reflected a little sadly that inevitably, some time in the future, they would be depending on me and I would let them down, and they would find out that their father, like all fathers, was no miracle worker after all and that he too had feet of clay. But looking at them now, I knew that the knowledge was safe for this time.

Just in front of my family was General Kosasih, then Gordon Reid in his wheelchair next to Mrs Waller, and

134

around them *Perth* survivors from all over Australia. As I was about to stand up one more face caught my eye. It was Sumantri's. He was attending the ceremony as the guest of the Australian Government who had readily agreed to invite him down, and I thought how fitting it was that this excellent fellow should be there.

As our eyes met he flashed the grin I'd got to know so well, and I smiled back. Then after taking a quick look behind me at the relics to reassure myself that I hadn't dreamt it all, I stood up to make the speech.

SUMATRA

STRAIT

"PERTH" ⊕
"HOUSTON" ⊕

TOPPERS I.

MERAK

SANGIAN I.

BANTEN
BAY

SUNDA

SERANG ●

KRAKATAU I.

WEST